"VOICES
IN THE
BIG SKY!"

**A CONCISE HISTORY
OF RADIO AND TELEVISION IN MONTANA
FROM THE 1920's TO THE PRESENT**

C HOWARD MCDONALD
AUTHOR

**Brought to you by
BIG M Broadcast Services
Post Office Box 1672
BOZEMAN, MT 59715**

Published by BIG M Broadcast Services
Bozeman, Montana

First Edition
First Printing-500-January 1996
Library of Congress Catalog Card Number 95-96195

ISBN 1-57502-109-9

Frontpiece printed by permission from the
Museum of the Rockies, Bozeman MT
Ed Craney Mural photograph courtesy
Ronald Cass—KXLF-TV

KSCO Studio photograph courtesy
American Radio Brokers, Inc.

Additional copies may be obtained by
mailing the order form found at the back of the book.

Also available on audio cassette voiced by the Author.

VOICES IN THE BIG SKY! may be obtained by retail
outlets at special rates.

Printed in the USA by

*M*ORRIS
PUBLISHING

3212 E. Hwy 30
Kearney, NE 68847
800-650-7888

Courtesy Museum of the Rockies, Bozeman, Montana.
From the Jim Masterson section of the Greater Montana Foundation
Collection.

~Dedication~
To my lovely wife, June, my four great children;
Don, Gary, Linda and Rick & my wonderful grandchildren;
Brandon, Brittany and Codi.

Your Husband, Dad and PaPa.

Contents

Charts Maps and Pictures

Forward

Recently someone asked Howard McDonald what he did before he was in radio and Howard said, "I was in high school." That sums it up and puts Howard's adult life into perspective: Radio! Not only has he done an exemplary job of researching this book, he has lived through at least half of the historic timeline.

When you meet Howard, you'll notice he has one of the greatest voices in the Big Sky. I remember hearing him for the first time on KGHL in Billings, Montana back in the 60's when I was still going to high school, desperately wanting to get into broadcasting, and wishing God would bless me with a deep, resonant voice such as Howard's. He was among my mentors and I pressed my nose against the control room window and watched with fascination while he performed radio magic.

Once he opened the control room to me, showed me how everything worked, and shared his knowledge and experience with me. My life was never the same afterwards. Ever since I signed on KUFM at the University of Montana in Missoula on that cold January 31, 1965, I have felt as though I was a contributor to the history Howard tells.

As you read "Voices in the Big Sky!" listen for the static and crackle in the night as the exciting chronicle of Montana's broadcasting history unfolds. It's being told by one of its creators.

Ronald D. Bradshaw
Former Operations Manager
KBIG, Billings

Preface & Acknowledgements

It would be extremely difficult to determine exactly when the idea for this treatise began! It is a project that was in the back of my mind for many years and perhaps had its beginnings during a period when research was started for a paper to be submitted to the Greater Montana Foundation.

Since then a wealth of information has come to my attention, both in verbal and written form. Many sources have been tapped in the preparation of "Voices in the Big Sky!"

It would be next to impossible to list them all. It is my hope the bibliography and this preface will suffice, even though they are both inadequate and fail to give all credit where it is due!

E. B. "Ed" Craney, a long-time broadcaster and pioneer gave much assistance through a series of tape recordings that dealt with his many and varied experiences during the early days of Montana Radio and TV.

Minnie Paugh, now retired, formerly overseer of the Special Collections Department of the Renne Library at Montana State University at Bozeman, made the files on broadcast stations available and offered both interest and encouragement.

Several members of my family deserve credit. Junie, my wife of over forty years, was wonderfully patient along the way and a great encouragement. She sacrificed personally by liquidating some of her own property to assist publication. Don, my oldest son, who is also a broadcaster, offered valuable technical input. My son, Gary, was literary advisor and cheering section.

I owe a great debt to Ron Richards, who, along with being a fine author and broadcaster, was a good friend for many years. His thesis was a valuable resource and the material is priceless. Many memories of him are precious as I recall our days as teenagers and the clandestine radio station we operated out of his recreation room on the southside of Missoula. This was before the area had a second radio station and we were able to give listeners within a few blocks of his home a "choice."

Montana airwaves are poorer without Ron "Pax" Richards since he departed this life in August 1990, at the young age of 56.

However, in spite of a wealth of input, much of the data that is enshrined herein comes from my own experience and memory, making it very difficult to offer outside documentation. Forty years of involvement in and association with broadcasting has left an indelible mark on both my mind and memory. Nearly thirty of those years have been spent in association with 14 of Montana's broadcast operations. Several of them are the pioneer stations in Montana.

I have also been honored to have a part in placing a new station on the air (KBOZ, 1975) and to be involved in the beginning stages of stations KKMT and KKMT-FM at Ennis, from the ground up! I am pleased we were able to bring the stations up to the construction stage without the assist of either consulting engineer or communications attorney.

My personal background as announcer, program director, manager and engineer, along with sales, has provided a wealth of knowledge concerning the state's broadcast industry.

While it has been impossible to cover all aspects of our BIG SKY country's broadcast history, it is my hope the information offered here will be valuable to both historians and broadcasters, and will be even a little entertaining along the way. May Montana Broadcasting be better because of it, rather than in spite of it

> Howard McDonald
> The Radio Ranch
> 1996

"........their sound went into all the earth
and their words unto the ends of the world.

(Romans 10:18 KJV)

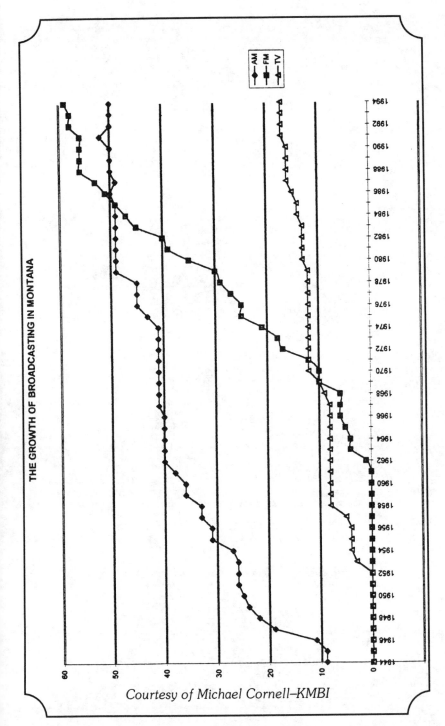

THE GROWTH OF BROADCASTING IN MONTANA

Courtesy of Michael Cornell–KMBI

xi

1

"In The Beginning"

Montanans are a history minded people. Even a cursory survey of the shelves of any major library in the state reveals a wealth of books dedicated to telling the Montana story or some portion of it. The Montana Historical Society, founded in the state's earliest days, bulges with artifacts and documents from the Big Sky Country's past.

The classic tales of the Treasure State, such as the Vigilantes, Gold Rush days, conflicts of the Copper Kings, the early days of statehood, trappers and cowboys along with the discovery and development of the grand Yellowstone region have been told and retold.

However, there are at least two areas in Montana history that have not been adequately reported by historians: transportation and communications.[1] While this treatise will not attempt to document all aspects of the state's communications industry, we will focus on at least some of the more significant events in the history of radio and television broadcasting within the past seventy-five to eighty years.

Very little is in print concerning Montana's broadcasting stations. Ronald P. Richards, in his master's thesis at the University of Montana, documented the early days of the Treasure State's broadcasters,[2] but the work was not published and therefore was not circulated. Brier and Blumberg[3] devoted two chapters to broadcasters, but both simply began to scratch the surface. Malone and Roeder, in their monumental work, assigned two paragraphs to broadcasting, mentioning two pioneer radio stations and one early television outlet.[4]

While this work is by no means exhaustive, an attempt will be made to document Montana broadcasting's post World War I evolution, as well as the advents of FM and TV following the Second World War, along with the many and varied developments of the present era.

At the close of 1995, government records showed 138 broadcasting stations (AM, FM and TV) in Montana, including construction permits at various points.[5] This is in sharp contrast to the days sixty years ago when radio stations existed only in the major cities, each community able to support only a single broadcast outlet. Montana was the last state in the

Union to be authorized an FM station, yet when its first AM (KDYS) began, only 38 others were on the air in the United States.[6]

No one knows when the first radio signals originated in the state. In the years between 1916 and the early 1920s, various radio experimenters or amateurs, both licensed and clandestine, filled the airwaves with an assortment of squeaks, squawks, whistles and whines, and on occasion, some music or speech. It was a wide-open era, and the Federal government had just started controlling communications, but had little, if any authority to enforce regulation of the new medium called radio.

However, radio historians have determined that experimental radio signals were sent from an area near Stevensville as early as 1919. Ashley C. Dixon, a local banker who had moved from Chicago, reportedly set up a radio transmitter at his Ravalli County home near the "Three Mile" Trading Post and was broadcasting local musical talent and talk. This endeavor was short-lived and came to an end when Dixon moved to Spokane. The station, like many others of its time, was never licensed and no records were kept of the broadcasts.[7]

Other unlicensed broadcasters followed in Dixon's footsteps all across Montana.

The history of Montana is vague concerning many of the early-day licensed stations. Then, as now, the Federal government kept no records of deleted facilities, and it fell to the newspapers to document pioneer broadcast endeavors and record them for posterity. Unfortunately, the papers seldom mentioned anything except their own broadcast undertakings.

From the beginning, broadcasting in Montana has been different! The immense distances and small population made both radio and TV a real challenge. In a state with an area of 147,138 square miles and less than one-half million population, radio began in the 1920s on very shaky and unstable ground. Only Alaska offered a greater challenge to broadcasters.

An early-day radio map indicated there were several stations on the air in the years around 1922. The map showed KFBB at Havre, along with KFBF at Butte and KFCH in Billings. KFBF was reportedly licensed to the "Butte School of Telegraphy," but nothing else is known about the school or station.[8] There have been reports of a KFBA operating at Butte in the 1920s, but this was probably a misprint of the KFBF call letters. KGIR was the first permanent radio station in the Mining City.

KFCH, a station promoted by the Billings Gazette, began November 7th, 1922 and lasted at least into the following month when all references to the station disappeared from the newspaper's radio page.[9]

About the same time, the call sign KFED was issued to the Billings Polytechnic Institute (now Rocky Mountain College) for an experimental station.[10] It is doubtful the station ever broadcast more than test programs in the form of phonograph records for the benefit of students who built radio receivers in a class at the Institute.

Controversy has arisen in recent years concerning the "first" radio station in Montana. Today, KEIN at Great Falls (formerly KFBB) uses the slogan, "Montana's First Radio Station," and letterheads for KFBB carried this motto for many years. Available documentation indicates KFBB/KEIN is the oldest station in the state, but was not the first.

The claim has been made that a station using the call letters KFDO, operating out of Bozeman, was the first in Montana, but little or no real documentation has been offered. The station reportedly received responses "from every state in the Union," and was "operated by Everett Cutting who acted as engineer, business manager, trouble shooter and announcer."[11]

Several old-timers in the Bozeman area recall that in the early '20s, a station was operating out of the living room of a fellow who lived in the Sourdough section of Bozeman. This station reportedly used the call sign KBOZ, but no records have been found to indicate it was ever licensed. There is a possibility the early-day KBOZ was the successor to KFDO.[12]

Nearly every Montana city had some sort of pioneer broadcasting station. Most of them were never licensed and ceased operation after a short time. A clandestine station operated out of the Wilma Building in downtown Missoula, sometime in 1923. The station's demise came during a local political broadcast when the participants became so rowdy and obscene the police confiscated the transmitter, put the station off the air and the operators in the county jail. Radio transmitters were simple to build in those years, and many unlicensed stations operated for a short while in nearly all Montana's major cities and towns.

+KDYS+

KDYS at Great Falls, was in every sense, Montana's pioneer broadcast station. Under the sponsorship of the Great Falls *Tribune* and its publisher, O. S. Warden, KDYS opened officially at 7:30pm on May 19, 1922, to become the first station in the state to be licensed by the Federal Government. Test broadcasts the previous week resulted in a number of reception reports, including one from as far away as Los Angeles.

The actual dedicatory broadcast on the 19th generated reports from the states of California, Idaho, Utah and Nevada, causing the *Tribune* to boast in the next morning's edition

"...........in its initial program, the Tribune's radio station blazed the trail of wireless telephony in the Intermountain states........-

reports came from lonely cabins in the heart of the mountains, where the program was heard plainly."[13]

Following opening remarks by *Tribune* publisher Warden, the station offered a musical program that was interrupted by a voltage drop in the city's power system. There were also problems with some of the hastily constructed receivers around the city.

In spite of the early problems, KDYS went on a regular schedule the following day, Sunday the 20th, that featured a service from First Christian Church in Great Falls in the morning, and a bedtime story program at 7:45 in the evening. Both programs became mainstays in the new station's schedule for its 18 month lifetime.

The daily schedule was always abbreviated by modern standards, but featured many "live" programs that originated in the KDYS studios at the *Tribune* office building, where the customary "flat top" antenna was perched on the building's roof, between two poles. At times, the city's phone system was over loaded by listeners calling in requests to the performers.

KDYS, along with KFBB at Havre, which began in the fall of 1922, broadcast one of the first "remotes" in Montana radio history. Both stations aired the Dempsey-Gibbons boxing match that was staged in Shelby on July 4, 1923. However, this was no co-operative effort. Each station sent staff members to the fight scene, and the individual broadcasts were sent to the respective stations over telephone lines.

While KDYS operated only three or four days a week with accompanying promotion and program schedules in the *Tribune*, the offerings were very consistent until about October 1, 1923. Then, the station, for all practical purposes, ceased broadcasting due to equipment problems, spawned by the lack of components for the transmitter. About this time, the *Tribune* announced the station would be silent about 10 days "for repair." On November 25, a news story clearly indicated the station might return in six months, but cautioned that the resumption of the broadcasts would "depend upon the state of affairs in the radio world."[14]

KDYS never returned to the air, and Great Falls did not see the resumption of local radio until September 1929 when KFBB moved to the city from Havre. However, this short-lived endeavor made the residents of the Electric city aware of radio and paved the way for KFBB and others.

The Tribune did not venture into radio again until 1948 when they were part of the endeavor that spawned KMON. Had KDYS prospered and remained on the air, Montana radio history might have been very different. KFBB probably would not have moved to Great Falls, and may have been the station that perished instead of KDYS. As Great Falls' pioneer radio station, KDYS might have ventured into television in the

1950s in place of KFBB. However, speculation profits little. The KDYS call sign was never used by another station in the U-S-A.

Newspaper ownership of radio stations was a pattern that began early in the history of Broadcasting in the United States and has continued into modern times. Some examples are: WGN (*Chicago Tribune*), WQXR (*New York Times*), KSD (*Saint Louis Post-Dispatch*), KRON (*San Francisco Chronicle*), WMT (*Waterloo, Iowa Morning Tribune*) and KOWH (*Omaha World-Herald*). In Montana, it was not a popular combination except for the *Tribune's* early association with KDYS and their later affiliation with KMON, along with the *Miles City Star's* ownership of KRJF (later KATL).

+KFBB+

In October of 1922, several months after the beginning of KDYS, F. A. Buttrey opened KFBB at Havre on the top floor of his department store. The home manufactured transmitter had a rated power of fifty watts and fed the antenna atop the store.[15] The station's first broadcasts were intermittent, but once things got on a regular schedule, it was credited with having been "constantly in service for more than 2,600 days, a record unequalled by few stations."[16] The first broadcasts were mainly weather and market reports, along with some music, mostly on phonograph records.[17]

Buttrey moved KFBB to Great Falls in 1929. He believed the larger market would offer more opportunity for service and station revenue. Havre did not have local radio service again until 1947 with the advent of KOJM.

In spite of contrary predictions, Buttrey's station prospered in Great Falls, and became an integral part of the community and area. For a time, the relocated station maintained studios at the old Park Hotel in downtown Great Falls, a site that was later used by its first competitor, KXLK. The two steel towers were erected on the hotel roof, with the station's "clothesline" antenna strung between them. In later years, when the studios were moved to the First National Bank building, the transmitter was located west of the city on the Vaughn highway. A residence next door to the transmitter building served as a home for the station engineer.

In 1936, after many years of offering either locally produced or syndicated programs on acetate discs, KFBB became a part of the Columbia Broadcasting System (CBS), and maintained that affiliation until 1961, when the management felt the station was "tied too close" to the network. In the years between, KFBB kept high standards of local programming, and developed its famous "Farmer's Noon Hour," which is discussed in another section of this treatise. For a while, in the years before network affiliation, KFBB produced its own soap-opera. It was entitled "Frank and

Mary Stubblefield," and was made up of local talent as well as several KFBB staff members.

+KUOM+

As radio began to develop, educational institutions saw the potential for the medium as an extension of their instructional programs. However, due to long-standing pressure from the commercial broadcasters, very few educational AM stations have survived to the present day. When the present FM broadcast band was established in 1945, the FCC sought to solve the problem by allocating a portion of the band to strictly educational use (88 to 92 mHz). Many pioneer educationals on the AM band were either pushed off the air or forced to share time with one or more commercial stations.

In the 1920s, educational stations proliferated to the point where there were nearly 200 on the air, nationwide. By the close of the decade, nearly all had given up, or had been forced out of business.[18]

The University of Montana entered the educational radio field in 1925 with KUOM. Montana's pioneer educational station was responsible for many firsts in state broadcasting, including Montana's initial political broadcasts; among them one that featured Alfred E. Smith, the Democrat contender for President. KUOM proved to be innovative in bringing educational programs to the state, but also provided live classical music and popular fare on a regular basis. The University station was probably the first in the state to do a re-creation of a sports event from a distant city, broadcasting a basketball game from Bozeman, 200 miles away.

Doctor C. D. Shallenberger, head of the University Physics Department, was the guiding hand through KUOM's lifetime.

In spite of plans for a state-wide hookup with studios at each unit of the Montana University System and a high-powered transmitter near Lewistown, in the exact center of the state, the license for KUOM was allowed to expire at the end of 1929 because of financial cutbacks by the state legislature.[19] KUOM was truly a victim of the Depression.

The call sign KUOM was later assigned to the University of Minnesota at Minneapolis. At present, each unit of the University System has radio facilities, except for Western Montana College at Dillon. Montana State University at Bozeman has its own educational TV station, KUSM, operated by the school's Film and Television department.

+KGCX+

In the years following the advents of KDYS, KFBB and KUOM other state broadcasters came on the scene. Eastern Montana's first radio station was not a high powered, pretentious operation, located in one of the larger cities. Rather, it began in the back room of a bank in the small community of Vida, population approximately 25 souls.[20]

E.E. Krebsbach, a young bank clerk, and a friend, Joe Jacobs, fashioned a small seven and one-half watt radio transmitter in the fall of 1926 while awaiting authority from the Department of Commerce. The station was assigned the call letters KGCX, and began shortly after the authorization came in the mail on October 5, 1926. Vida is one of the smallest towns in the United States to ever be granted a commercial radio station license.

"Ed" Krebsbach located the KGCX studio in the back room of the First State Bank of Vida and operated on an intermittent basis when he was not needed "up front." Besides being a farmer and banker, Krebsbach was a tinkerer and a musician, two talents that probably lead to his interest in radio. Ed was very proficient on the saxophone and was much in demand at dances throughout the area.

KGCX did not prosper financially at Vida and most of the funds for the station's operation came out of Krebsbach's own pocket. He had dreams of moving the station to a larger town, and Wolf Point was up the road about 25 miles. There he hoped to find more merchants that would be willing to advertise to a larger population. Besides, the government would not authorize more power for KGCX unless it was licensed to a larger community.

In 1929 Krebsbach received permission to move the station to Wolf Point where they were welcomed by the local commercial club or Chamber of Commerce. Much of the money for the move and upgrading of the station was raised through popular subscription along with donations from the club. On August 21, 1929, KGCX officially opened at Wolf Point after being off the air for several months.

From the beginning, the station showed an interest in sports broadcasting. During the early-days at Vida, the station broadcast sports events from Poplar, a town fifty miles away. With the relocation to Wolf Point, the station began covering local basketball and even did a "recreation" of the 1929 World Series using a local announcer at the Western Union Office. Throughout the years, KGCX has maintained its sports coverage, not only for Sidney, but also the various surrounding communities.

In 1933 the Radio Corporation of America (RCA) published a multicolor map that promoted radio listening across the United States and showed the stations that were operating at that time.

The map was called, "The Radio Waves are Calling," and asked the readers, "Have you ever wanted to visit California, New York, Texas, Illinois, Florida, Montana or any of the other 42 states in the Union? Would you like to spend tonight in Canada or Mexico?"

The map's copy went on to proclaim that Americans were increasingly taking "tours" of the nation by listening to their radios and bringing in stations and programs from distant points. The practice of listening for distant stations became known as "DXing," from the radio amateur term for distance (DX).

The purpose of the map and accompanying text was to promote RCA radios and parts.

While the map showed all 605 stations on the air at that time, it listed Montana among the six states it called attention to within the text. However, it went even further:

"What will it be tonight? Hollywood, Wolf Point, Tupelo or New York?"

Evidently, when KGCX was in operation at Wolf Point in the 1930s, it was considered "quite a find" among DXers who combed the radio band at night, looking for distant stations.[21]

At that time, KGCX probably broadcast, especially at night, with no more than 500 watts and was assigned to a frequency (channel) that was occupied by many other stations across the country. Being in the Mountain Time zone, KGCX was probably still on the air after Eastern and Central zone stations signed off for the night.

Initially, KGCX prospered at Wolf Point, attracting a large number of sponsors in the area, all eager to advertise. However, the Depression years caused the number of sponsors to dwindle and the station fell on hard times.

Throughout the lean years, much of the support for KGCX came from local benefits such as dances and "pot-luck" suppers. Listeners were also among the contributors that helped keep the station on the air. The 1930s were hard in the Wolf Point area, even as the rest of the nation began to move out of the Depression. Advertising support did not recover at Wolf Point and Krebsbach anticipated another move, this time as before, to a larger community. Ed found his new home in nearby Sidney, a town that was supposedly "Depression proof."

By September 1942 the station was on the air from a new site near Sidney, with studios downtown. During the war years, KGCX kept listeners up-to-date with local happenings as well as news from the European and Pacific areas. This was accomplished by a very unique arrangement whereby the station utilized an "off-the-air" pickup from a station in Canada that was affiliated with the Canadian Broadcasting Corporation (CBC). At the end of World War II, the station affiliated with the U-S based Mutual Broadcasting System (MBS). Another post war improvement was a power increase as the station went to 5,000 watts at 1480 kHz. At about the same time, KGCX opened studios and offices in the nearby community of Williston, North Dakota.

KGCX's success has been both financial and in the realm of service to the area. So much so, that other stations in the Northeastern Montana area have attempted to capitalize on the success of KGCX with call signs such as KCGM (Scobey) and KVCK (Wolf Point), which sound like KGCX.

In 1994 it was reported that KGCX and its FM companion, KGCH, had left the air because of financial difficulties and management problems. There has been no notice of their revival. A Montana broadcast pioneer station has apparently suffered a premature death.

+KGEZ+

Northwestern Montanans were without local radio service until late February 1927 when KGEZ at Kalispell, using a five watt transmitter, went on the air from the Elks Temple. The initial broadcast was a play-by-play of a High School basketball tournament, a first for any Montana station.

The tournament was, for all purposes, a test program for KGEZ. The actual opening broadcast occurred on March 21, 1927 with a variety of offerings, such as stock and weather reports, a little music from the new station's few records, along with correct time signals. The station was fortunate in having an immediate group of advertisers.[22]

As the station grew, and became a regular part of the community, Donald Treloar, a friend of the owner, became involved more and more in the station and became the manager. The station was moved to Treloar's home on South Fourth Avenue in Kalispell. Eventually, the station ended up in the First National Bank Building, with a new transmitter site south of town near the broadcast plant occupied by the station today.[23]

Several features of KGEZ made it unique among early-day Montana stations. Following the 1927 debut, the station petitioned the government for a power of 100 watts, a feature the station maintained into the early 1950s. Before the station finally increased its power to the FCC standard of 250 watts allowed Class IV stations, it was the last full-time 100 watt outlet in the United States. Today, KGEZ operates with 5,000 watts at 600 kHz.

KGEZ was also the last pioneer Montana radio station to seek affiliation with a national network. It was the late 1940s before the station ceased to be an independent broadcast endeavor.

+KGHL+

In 1924 when Charles O. Campbell of the Northwestern Auto Supply Company of Billings decided to add a line of radio receivers to his many other products, no one could envision it would have far reaching effects on the history of Montana radio.

The sale of the unwieldy radio receivers was not only complicated by the massive size of the receiving unit and its huge battery package, but there were no local radio stations in the area. There was very little motivation for a salesman to haul a receiver to a residence or farm home for a demonstration if there were no stations to receive.

At night, there was fairly good reception in the Billings area, but the daytime hours were a salesman's nightmare. There was simply no reliable reception. KFBB at Havre was not powerful enough to be heard in Billings, and the only station that reached the area was KFKX at Hastings, Nebraska, a station that picked up the programming from KDKA at Pittsburgh via a short-wave link and relayed it into the Midwest. And, unless conditions were just right, KFKX was not always there.

Campbell figured there was a simple answer to the problem. Build a radio station! He did just that, with the result being KGHL, which began regular broadcasting on June 8, 1928. A 250 watt transmitter was fabricated in Denver, shipped to Billings and installed at the palatial Northwestern Auto/KGHL studio building on North Broadway. The station's "clothesline" antenna was installed on the roof of the office building.

KGHL's opening broadcast, which began at 7 o'clock on the evening of June 8th, featured a variety of carefully screened and auditioned local talent, along with an address by Montana's Governor, J. E. Erickson, from his office in the Executive Mansion, 250 miles away in Helena.

In the beginning, KGHL's programming began at 7 am with a variety of music, time signals, weather forecasts, market summaries and newscasts. The noon hour was highlighted by a remote organ broadcast from a local theatre. Afternoons were much the same as mornings with book reviews and household hints added. The station was silent each evening from 8 until 11 pm, probably to allow local listeners to enjoy "DX" reception from distant places.

KGHL paid off almost immediately, both from the sale of Campbell's receivers and advertising time. When the local newspaper, the *Billings Gazette*, offered to lease the station, Campbell refused. The paper then threatened to build their own station and force KGHL out of business, but that never materialized. KGHL was alone in the Billings market until 1946.[24]

Improvements and power increases came regularly to KGHL. By 1930 the station was radiating 1,000 watts, and the transmitter was moved six miles outside the city on the road to Laurel, where it operated at 950 on the dial. In 1938, permission was granted for 5,000 watts and the station moved to its present dial position of 790 kHz in March of 1941. KGHL's huge 568 foot self-supporting tower was for many years the tallest structure of its kind in the United States.[25]

Another significant KGHL milestone was the affiliation with the National Broadcasting Company in 1931, a relationship that lasted into the 1980s.

Campbell always managed to get in a plug for the parent business. On each station break, it was, "KGHL, Billings, The Northwestern Auto Supply Company Station."

The station, which demanded on-the-air perfection, was not without problems elsewhere. It was very difficult to convince eastern advertising agencies and timebuyers that with 5,000 watts, KGHL was able to cover all of Eastern Montana, Northern Wyoming and a good portion of the Dakotas, an area that came to be known as the "Midland Empire."[26]

During World War II, the National Broadcasting Company's radio network featured a news commentator named Larry Smith. Smith's propagandizing against the Axis Powers (Japan and Germany) made it necessary that he not be accessible to Nazi or Japanese sympathizers. Smith originated his daily news commentary program secretly from the KGHL studios for several months during the war.

KGHL has always been one of Montana's prestige stations. If there is one station in Montana that has stood head and shoulders above the others, it is KGHL. The familiar voices of Eric Thornton, Ed Yocum, Harry Turner, Cy Taylon, Maury White, Jack Bogut, Bob Leinweber, Warren Kemper, Bill Zaputil, Norm Wegmet, Don Gaye and the author were a vital part of Central and Southern Montana households for many years.

The classic N-B-C chimes, followed by the unique station indentification: "This is Billings......KGHL," told listeners they were in tune with a friend and neighbor. Some of the old-time announcers were accused of slurring the call letters to give the impression they were saying, "Cagy as Hell!"

In recent years, KGHL has received many awards, including "Country Music Station of the Year," several years in a row. In 1986 the station and its FM affiliate, KIDX, sold for $3,000,000.

+KGIR+

Like many Montana stations, KGIR at Butte came into being through the efforts of one man. In this instance, the man behind the station was Edmund Blodgette "Ed" Craney.

Ed Craney was born in Washington State, but spent many of his growing up years on an island in the middle of Montana's Swan Lake at the home of his father, who was a lumberman and railroad builder. The island could only be reached by steamboat and young Edmund was offered his early schooling by various women in his family, including his mother, sister and a lady who eventually became his sister-in-law.[27]

Fresh out of a Spokane high school where he had been advertising manager for the school newspaper, young Craney's expectations to obtain a college education were set aside when he encountered Tom Symons, a former advertiser who operated an aviation school. Craney had planned to work in the woods with his father's timber operation for a summer and then pursue a degree at Washington State College. His mother had encouraged him to become a doctor, while he had set his own sights on becoming an electrical engineer.[28]

Symons also owned a radio parts store and offered young Craney a position with that firm. He accepted the offer, but soon realized there was little demand for radio because there were no radio stations in Spokane.[29] Craney decided to build his own station, with Symons as a partner. The result was KFDC (later KFPY), which began in 1922.

Craney continued his involvement in the radio parts firm, which had expanded into the wholesale end of the business. A sales trip brought him to Butte, where there was also no radio station, except for a "ham" or amateur operator named Grey, who played phonograph records on the air for an hour or two each day.[30] Craney decided to build a station in the Butte area. Leaving Symons to run KFDC, he applied for a license from the Federal Radio Commission and set out to build the station.[31]

Following a series of roadblocks, mainly engineered by the Montana Power Company and its corporate twin, the Anaconda (Copper) Company, Ed set up operations in Shiner's Furniture Store in uptown Butte.[32] The Radio Commission issued the call letters KGIR to the station and Craney went on the air the evening of January 21, 1929. The fledgling station's antenna was strung between two poles, one atop Shiner's store and the other on the Miner's Union Hall, across the street. At the time, it was the "highest" (above sea level) radio antenna in the United States.

The initial broadcast began at 6 o'clock in the evening with "The Star Spangled Banner," followed by an ecumenical religious service with George Finnegan, Catholic Bishop from Helena; Charles Cole, pastor of Butte's Mountain View Methodist Church and an invocation by Emmanuel Sternheim, the Rabbi of the Mining City's Jewish congregation.

The broadcast that followed lasted for 12 hours. Butte was a 24 hour town in those days. The local talent included Jimmie Nettle with a vocal solo, a series of recitations by the students of Mrs. Walter Orton and Madame Marie Leipheimer, the Steward Warner Sales Variety Show, Butte Male Chorus, Butte Miner's Band, the Phil Thomas Orchestra and many other contributions, including Charlie Erb's Entertainers, a group from a local saloon that had a questionable reputation.[33]

The debut of KGIR was reported the next morning in the local press:

> "The Butte program was heard in all parts of the country and more than 1,000 telegrams were received from the midwest states, the intermountain territory and the Pacific Coast. Hundreds of visitors stood outside the glass enclosed studio on the fourth floor of Shiner's last night and looked on as some of the best talent in Butte and Anaconda stood before the microphone. E. B. Craney, the manager of the station, encouraged by the hundreds of telephone calls and telegrams which began to arrive early in the evening, spent a few moments expressing his gratitude."[34]

However, nearly a month before, the same newspaper reported the anticipated advent of KGIR in terms not quite so complementary:

> "Broadcasting from KGIR, Butte's newest radio station, will have practically no effect on reception from the larger stations which are heard here. KGIR is at a congested spot on the dial."[35]

Both local newspapers made offers to purchase the station the day it signed on, but Craney politely refused to sell KGIR.

Craney's chief crony and compatriot in KGIR's early days was Leo "Mac" McMullen, who had been a hoist operator in the mines and before the beginning of KGIR was the head of a local ice company that was feeling the pinch of the refrigerator era. Mac became the station chief salesman, assistant manager and storyteller.[36]

"E.B." as Craney came to be known, was always ready to "do battle," whether it was a problem with the local labor unions boycotting his local advertisers because of some imagined injustice, or the Anaconda Company threatening to shut down the *Montana Standard's* Anaconda edition if the station persisted in operating a studio in that city.

Craney, supposedly wise to the idiosyncrasies of the Mining City, received an education from McMullen one evening when Mac pointed out to him that a series of "musical dedications" he was making on an evening request program were actually "availability" announcements for the local "ladies of the night."[37]

During the early days, Craney and his wife often ran the station by themselves, especially in the early morning hours. The tale has been told, denied and told again, that one early morning, Ed and the Missis got into a heated argument in the studio while a record was playing on the air. During the shouting match, the microphone switch was pushed into the "on" position, and a good portion of the tiff was broadcast, including some very "choice" words used by the very proper Mrs. Craney, words that were usually reserved for the boys in the mines. Many listeners began phoning their friends until the whole town and surrounding area was enjoying "Life With the Craneys" on KGIR.[38]

Because of their mutual interest in broadcasting, Craney became a good friend of Montana's controversial Senator Burton K. "Bolshevik Burt" Wheeler. E. B.'s detractors maintained for years that Wheeler was the real power and finance source behind the Craney empire, but this was probably untrue. However, Wheeler was always ready to "go to bat" for Craney in many of his struggles, such as the battle to keep NBC from cancelling its affiliation with Montana stations during the Depression.

As he expanded, Craney became known more and more as "E.B." or "Mr. Craney." He formulated a "policy book" which was the operations "bible" for his Z Bar Net stations. Every male employee was required to wear a necktie while on duty, even though the studio might be unbearably hot and even if engineering or maintenance duties were being performed.[39] The rumor persisted that Ed wore a suit and tie to bed.

Ed lived next door to the KGIR studios at Nissler Junction west of Butte and was able to drop into the station for a visit, day or night. Even though he was genuinely concerned about the operation, Craney always checked to see if the operator on duty was wearing a tie.[40]

Much of the history of KGIR is contained in other sections of this treatise. See section; "There was a fellow by the name of Craney." Edmund B. Craney, the last of the Montana broadcast pioneers, recently passed away at his home in Saint George, Utah.

+KGVO+

For many years, aspiring young radio buffs in Montana were told the story of Arthur J. "Art" Mosby being kicked off a freight train in the rail yards in Missoula, only to be left penniless and stranded in the Garden City. The story is probably apocryphal, but it seems certain the man who founded KGVO probably arrived in Missoula with little in his pocket and high hopes in his heart and mind. It never hurt that he married into the Greenough family, either.

Mosby, or "A.J." as he came to be called, founded one of Montana's first electrical shops and subsequently purchased from his brother one of the first radio transmitters in Montana.[41] The home-brew unit had been used by KUOM and at least one clandestine station in the Missoula area.

By 1930, following the demise of KUOM and a few other short-lived and unlicensed radio stations, it was apparent that "radio reception was not good enough to encourage the sale of radio receivers."[42] One of the mainstays of the Mosby electrical shop was receiving sets and the many associated parts, which were not selling. A.J. decided to build a radio station, applied to the Federal Radio Commission and waited for permission to build.

KGVO, Missoula's first licensed commercial station, began the 17th of January, 1931.

The station was authorized several months before the January sign on, and suffered several delays in getting on the air. The new station's first transmitter was assembled by the Mosby electrical shop from the shop's assortment of new parts, ordered by mail, selected pieces from the retired transmitter of KFBB,[43] a few parts from a cannibalized radio receiver and several huge meters that were rumored to have come from a discarded transmitter at WLW in Cincinnati, Ohio.

Construction of KGVO began in December 1930 and continued up to nearly the last moment of opening day. The initial broadcast began with an address by W. H. Beacon, the mayor of Missoula. The remainder of the six hour broadcast consisted of a hodge podge of local talent with people jamming the halls of the studio building to either see the broadcast or become a part of it.

When regular broadcasts began the following day, KGVO dipped into the local talent pool for much of the programming, supplementing with phonograph records.[44]

Initially, KGVO was a low-power affair, with its 100 watt transmitter feeding a long wire antenna between two poles on top of the roof of the Missoula Mercantile building, across the alley from the KGVO studios. However, following the Depression, power was increased and the station changed frequency. Those changes made it necessary to move the transmitter to a building located west of town on the main highway. In the 1950s, the transmitter was moved south of town and the building became part of the Bud Lake Truck Stop. It has since been demolished.[45]

From these humble beginnings, KGVO grew to become the leading radio station in Western Montana. In 1939 the station moved its studios to West Front Street. The new plant was described as "a broadcasting show place," and, "the best west of the Mississippi River."[46] Unfortunately, the palatial studio building burned on February 19, 1950 and was not restored until 1956.[47] In the interim, the station operated from its original address in Mosby's Union Block, a downtown office building that had been renamed the "Radio Central Building."

Until the middle 1970s, and in spite of two ownership changes, KGVO retained the slogan, "The Voice of the Five Great Valleys." The station moved from a lowly 100 watts in 1931 into their 1,000 watt era at 1420 kilohertz, beginning in 1936. Later, KGVO became a 5,000 watt daytime,

1,000 watt night time station at 1260 kHz, and finally found a permanent home at 1290 kHz during the great radio reallocation of March 29, 1941.

KGVO was one of the first stations in the northwest to hire a full time news director. The station was blessed with the early-day talents of John Rolfson, who was for many years the chief correspondent for ABC in Paris. ABC's Paul Harvey is a KGVO alumnus, spending two years there on his "way to the top" (see Harvey section).[48]

Art Mosby's daughter, Aline, was for many years a staff writer for United Press, International, both in the USA and several foreign bureaus. Mosby was enraged when Aline posed "topless" for a digest-sized scandal sheet in the 1950s. Aline and sister Mary Jane were partners in Mosby's KMSO-TV.

One newsman who worked at KGVO in the 1950s was forced to use a pseudonym on the air. He called himself Robert E. L. Martin. This supposedly kept him from being identified with his politics, but everyone in Missoula knew Martin was in reality Cyrus "Cy" Noe.

Another newsman, Don Weston, won several awards for the station, and served KGVO for many years until blindness brought an end to his illustrious career. Weston was very innovative and brought network calibre news reporting to Missoula and Western Montana. He was equally adept as a sportscaster. Many fine news reporters have come and gone at KGVO, but none of them would even attempt to fill the shoes of Don Weston. For many years he spearheaded and announced a special network from the capitol in Helena during Montana's legislative sessions. Somehow, the airwaves of Montana are not the same without Don Weston.

Stan Healey was an old-time newspaper reporter who worked many years for the *Missoulian*. When advancing years and personal problems brought Stan to loggerheads with the paper's management, he went to work for Weston at KGVO, covering the city beat he knew so well, and doing feature assignments. Healey occasionally went out on a limb and produced material on his own, hoping Weston would use it. He was paid by the "piece" and was not on a regular salary.

One morning, Stan headed up TV Mountain, where KMSO (TV) has their transmitter site. A four-wheel drive vehicle taking equipment and supplies to the site had gone off the road, about half-way up the mountain. The truck rolled and was smashed, but the driver survived without a scratch and was still at the scene when Healey arrived to do an on-the-spot interview.

Stan hauled his tape recorder and microphone back to the KGVO news room. When he rewound the tape, he discovered it was quite old and brittle. It broke in several places. Stan was in a frenzy! He had what he thought was a priceless story and asked one of the KGVO announcers to repair the tape while he got Weston's permission to use the story on the 11 pm news.

During the reassembly, the announcer put all the pieces back into the proper sequence, except the last one, which he spliced in backwards. In the rush to get the tape on the air, no one previewed it. All went well until it came to the tag line at the end of the story. It came out: "From TV Mountain, swen OVGK, Yelaeh Nats si siht!"

Weston kept the tape, and used it, complete with the reversed tag line, on his annual "Yearend Review of the News."

2

The Pre-War Trio

From January 1931 until October 1937, no new radio stations were constructed in Montana. The Great Depression and its aftermath made it difficult for the established stations and prevented the building of new ones. Consequently, several of Montana's larger cities were without local radio until the last half of the decade.

+KPFA+

In the late 1930s, Ed Craney of KGIR at Butte, determined to enlarge his sphere of influence and broadcasting range in Montana. His first thoughts were directed toward increasing the station's power to 50,000 watts, but in Montana this was neither practical nor allowable in the eyes of the FCC.

Besides, Craney had been in the forefront of the battle against the clear channels and other high-power stations. It would have been sheer hypocrisy for him to go that route. Instead, he envisioned a network of several 250 watt stations in other Montana cities, controlled by him, and programmed mainly from the Butte station.[49]

His first undertaking was KPFA at Helena. The FCC authorized the new station to operate on 1210 kHz (later 1240 kHz) with 250 watts. Along with the authorization, the Commission promised to keep a watchful eye on the Helena operation to make sure it would serve the Capital City and would not simply be a "slave" or repeater station for KGIR.

As he had done in Butte, Craney gathered outside investors that included Barclay Craighead, a prominent Montana politician and local businessman. KPFA went on the air as an NBC affiliate on October 1, 1937. Together with KGIR, it made up the Z Bar Net(work), which eventually grew to five stations.

Being located in Helena, KPFA was always the second flagship station of the Z Bar, and was the network's source for political news as well as public affairs programming that centered around state government.

The new station was located in the same building as the Helena office of United Press and the staff had only to go upstairs to get the latest news copy. The rustic log building that housed KPFA and the U-P was razed in recent years, but KPFA's successor, KBLL, maintains studios and offices just a few hundred yards east of the original KPFA self-supported tower, which is still used by KBLL.

+KRBM+

As soon as KPFA was on the air, Craney and his associates began work on KRBM at Bozeman. The station was destined to operate with 250 watts with the Craney engineers selecting 1420 as the frequency they would request in their petition to the FCC. KRBM was later moved to 1450 kHz, where it operates today as KMMS. Again, Craney took on local investors, including Robin B. MacNab of Bozeman, and his first manager, Pat Goodover, who was later an unsuccessful Republican candidate for the Montana governorship.

Initial plans for the Bozeman station were ambitious. They called for the studios to be located in the plush Baxter Hotel in downtown Bozeman, with the transmitting tower on the roof of the building. These plans met with immediate opposition from Bozeman residents. Aesthetics was the first issue, and there were many objections on those grounds, maintaining the tower would "spoil the beauty of the downtown area." Some felt the huge Baxter Hotel neon sign had already spoiled the landscape. However, the biggest complaint concerned safety. Many townspeople protested the plans, saying they were, "afraid the tower would fall on somebody, or something."

KRBM built a small brick structure east of the city on Highway Ten, hoping to install their transmitter there, and operate from the hotel. However, the "split" arrangement was deemed "too costly," and on the 15th of October, 1939, KRBM began broadcasting from the brick building. It was cramped, but it was used as a studio, office and transmitter building for almost 20 years. The planned arrangement in the Baxter was reduced to a small office, interview studio and mail drop for the station.

The beginning of World War II took many of the station's young and promising announcers. Therefore, Dorthea Neath, wife of the manager, was pressed into service and became one of Montana's first female announcers. George Davenport, a retired stage actor, who lived in Bozeman, was also used as an announcer during the war years at KRBM. Davenport was well known in the area as host of the Wednesday "Bank Night" at one of the local movie theatres.

For a time, KRBM was authorized by the FCC to identify as "KRBM, Bozeman-Livingston." This was dropped because the Livingston merchants failed to respond to the station's sales efforts there. Also, the station's frequency was so crowded at night they could barely be heard in Livingston.[50] Today, another station, KBOZ-FM, identifies as "Livingston-Bozeman."

+KRJF+

At the other end of the state, KRJF at Miles City began broadcasting just 94 days before the beginning of World War II. The war put an end to all construction and expansion of radio in the U-S-A.

KRJF was the child of the *Miles City Star*, the local newspaper, and began with 250 watts at 1340 on the dial on September 4, 1941. The studios were located on Miles City's Haines Street, near the local Country Club, in a building constructed especially for the new station.[51]

Because Miles City was a smaller city and due to the lack of concentration of population in Eastern Montana the new station was unable to secure network affiliation until after the war when they joined the Mutual Broadcasting System (MBS) in a package deal with KGCX at Sidney.

However, the station kept wartime listeners informed of the news of the day by securing a wire service. KRJF was one of the first radio stations in the state with a newswire, in an era when broadcasters were just beginning to use wire services legally. Up to that time, the newspapers had been in a constant battle to keep radio stations out of the news business. The new Miles City station kept listeners entertained with a variety of local musical programs along with syndicated drama and adventure programs. In 1954, KRJF became KATL, "The Cattle Call," and today operates with 10,000 watts at 770 on the dial.[52] The KATL call sign was "acquired" from a station in Houston, Texas.

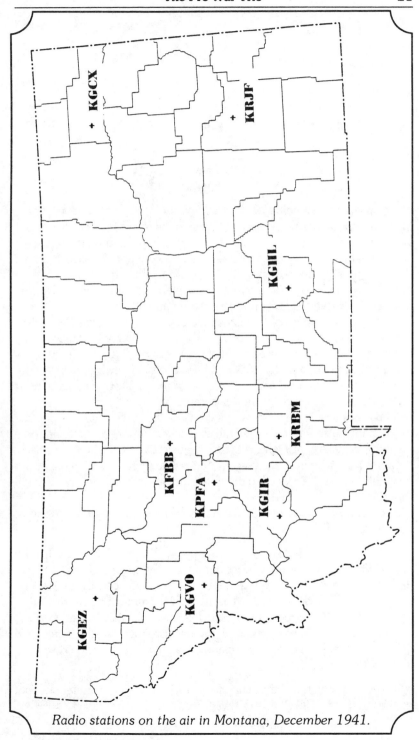

Radio stations on the air in Montana, December 1941.

3

Growing Pains

As broadcast technology developed and the number of receivers grew, Montana stations generally sought higher powers to serve the state's vast areas and "far between" communities. Yet, Montana broadcasters have been generally avid foes of the clear channel concept.[53] A clear channel station is one given exclusive rights to a particular frequency so as to provide wide coverage, both during the day and nighttime hours. No true clear channel stations remain today in the United States.

In the formative days of radio, the federal government generally authorized the power of stations according to the population of the station's city of license. This meant clear channel and other 50,000 watt frequencies could not even be allocated to Montana's largest cities. Beginning in the 1950s this was changed and today some of the highest powered stations in Montana are licensed to smaller communities.

Early Montana broadcasters, unable to obtain clear channels and the accompanying super power, felt the clears were infringing on their home territory, especially at night. If the high-powered stations were cut back, their frequencies could be used in states like Montana. If high power channels had been assigned to the state attitudes may have been much different.

Montana Senator Burton K. Wheeler spoke for some of the Montana broadcasters when he stated:

> "When (FCC Commissioner James L.) Fly began his term in 1939, he told me he was in favor of granting licenses for 10 or 12 'super-power' radio stations carrying some 500 thousand watts each. I opposed the idea. I pointed out that the super-power stations would have all the best programs and thus get all the business. A little station serving a community could not compete."[54]

It seems ironic that Ed Craney fought for years to keep stations "out in the sticks" off KGIR's 5,000 watt regional frequency of 1370.[55] No

Montana station has ever been assigned a Class I clear channel or given a three letter call sign. Three letter calls, such as KNX, were not issued after 1928. They had not only been assigned to broadcast stations, but also to maritime and police facilities. Most of the 1352 combinations were in use.

It was October 27, 1967 before the Treasure State had an AM station with power in excess of 5,000 watts. On that day KOFI at Kalipsell began broadcasting with 10,000 watts on 1180 kHz. Today, Montana has two 50 thousand watt stations, KOFI and KERR in Polson. KJJR at Whitefish, KGVW, Belgrade along with KATL and KMTA at Miles City all operate with 10,000 watts.

Following World War II, political pressure from the broadcasters caused restrictions on new stations to be lifted and out-dated regulations modernized to accommodate more stations on the broadcast band. This allowed radio service in many small communities for the first time. The tidal wave of new stations did not miss Montana.

Slightly over a year after the war ended, Billings' second radio station, KBMY signed on the air. This was Montana's first post-war station and began September 8, 1946. The new KBMY was quickly followed by KANA at Anaconda on November 6th of the same year.

KANA called attention to itself in the Montana Standard that day with an ad saying, "Music you'll like, no soap operas, 1230 kilocycles."[56]

In 1947, other Montana cities witnessed the beginning of their second radio stations. The year saw the advent of KBOW, Butte; KXLK, Great Falls and KXLL, Missoula. Radio service also came to other cities in 1947. The new stations were: KAVR and KOJM at Havre;[57] KXLO in Lewistown; KIYI, Shelby and KPRK at Livingston. The following year, new stations were established at Butte (KOPR), Great Falls (KMON) and Glendive (KXGN). A complete listing of Montana stations as they came on the air will be found in the Chronology section of this treatise.

Since 1946, at least one new radio or TV station has been started in Montana every year except 1952, 1956, 1960 and 1990. Stations have been authorized by the FCC for nearly every town with a population over 1,500. Permits have been issued for such communities as Belgrade (KGVW AM & FM), Scobey (KCGM), Red Lodge (KRBN) and West Yellowstone (KWYS).[58] On the ninth of October, 1986, the FCC authorized construction of a 10,000 watt daytime station on 710 kHz at Ennis, with a population of 700.[59] However, the station was not built due to a multitude of problems.

Along the way, consolidations have occurred. After World War II, two Great Falls broadcast permittees, the *Montana Farmer Stockman*, a *Great Falls Tribune* subsidiary, which held the construction permit for station KMFR, and a Salt Lake City multiple owner, permit holder for station KMON, merged their applications, keeping the KMON call letters and the more attractive KMFR frequency of 560 kHz. The construction of both stations was well underway when the merger took place.[60]

By 1964, it was apparent there was insufficient population and advertising revenue in Butte for three AM stations. Therefore, on August 16th of that year, KBOW and KOPR merged, with the resulting facility taking the KBOW call letters and studios along with the KOPR frequency (550 kHz) and transmitter site. The "New KBOW," under the management of former *Montana Standard* reporter "Shag" Miller, billed itself as "the highest powered radio station in Montana."[61] While the new KBOW probably had the best coverage in the state with its 5,000 watts at 550 kHz, it was not the most powerful. At that time, no station in Montana was operating in excess of 5,000 watts. Station KDBM at Dillon, a daytimer on 800 kHz, received FCC permission to move to the old KBOW frequency of 1490 kHz.

4

Remotes And Networks

In 1940, Montana had only eight radio stations. Broadcast facilities existed at Great Falls (KFBB-1290 kcs), Wolf Point (KGCX-1310 kcs), Kalispell (KGEZ-1310 kcs), Billings (KGHL-950 kcs), Butte (KGIR-1340 kcs), Missoula (KGVO-1260 kcs), Helena (KPFA-1210 kcs),[62] and Bozeman (KRBM-1420 kcs). KRJF at Miles City (1340 kcs) began in 1941. Most of the above frequencies were changed during the great radio reallocation of 1941.

In Montana, remote broadcasts and multiple station hookups were very common, even in the early days. KDYS and KFBB originated separate broadcasts of the Dempsy-Gibbons heavyweight fight from Shelby on July 4, 1923. KGHL featured a remote broadcast from the governor's office at the Executive Mansion in Helena during their first day on the air, June 8, 1928.[63] While still located in the small town of Vida, KGCX broadcast a high school basketball game from the town of Poplar, 50 miles away.[64]

Eventually, as telephone lines were upgraded to broadcast quality and costs reduced, nearly all Montana stations affiliated with one of the national networks. KGHL joined the National Broadcasting Company (NBC) on November 27, 1931. NBC originated a special hour-long broadcast to mark the occasion. KGIR at Butte had affiliated with NBC several months earlier and contributed to the program. KGVO and KFBB became new affiliates of the Columbia Broadcasting System (CBS) on the same day in 1936.[65]

KGCX at Wolf Point received permission to broadcast programs of the Canadian Broadcasting Corporation (CBC) until they were able to obtain affiliation with the Mutual Broadcasting System in 1946. This is the only instance in Broadcast history where a station in the United States affiliated with the CBC.[66] Also in 1946, KRJF became a Mutual affiliate. Only KGEZ remained without a national network affiliation into the late 1940s. The American Broadcasting Company (ABC), which was known as The Blue Network until 1945, had no fulltime affiliates in the state until 1948, but both the Z-Bar Net and KGHL carried some Blue Network programs on occasion in the late 1930s and early 1940s.[67]

There were several interconnections between Montana stations prior to 1937, mostly special hookups for election returns and special events, but most of them were temporary and have escaped accurate documentation.

The state's first fulltime network was the Z Bar Net, a combination of KGIR at Butte and KPFA in Helena, beginning in 1937.[68] KRBM at Bozeman was added in 1939. In the network's early days, KPFA and KRBM originated a minimum of local programming. The majority of the broadcast fare came from either NBC or the KGIR studios. Most of the national and regional commercial announcements also originated at KGIR and were fed to the other stations on the NBC network lines.

The new Z Bar Net instituted a few innovative concepts, including the use of reversible lines between the stations. These semi-high quality telephone lines were wired in a manner that allowed program material to be fed into either end, or termination, of the line and be received at the opposite end, simply by throwing a switch. This allowed for weather reports from each of the stations at the conclusion of the KGIR newscasts as well as an occasional program or announcement from KPFA or KRBM.[69] As mentioned earlier, KPFA originated several daily newscasts for Z Bar.

On Thanksgiving Day, 1946, the Z Bar stations adopted an "XL" (excel) prefix as the second and third letters of their call signs. KGIR became KXLF, KPFA changed to KXLJ and KRBM converted to KXLQ.[70] Stations KXLK at Great Falls and KXLL, Missoula were added in 1947.[71] Ed Craney, chief stockholder of the Z Bar, envisioned a vast radio network, spanning the Northwest, with stations in Portland (KXL), Ellensburg, Washington (KXLE) and Spokane (KXLY), linked with the five Z Bar Net stations.[72] KXLE had previously been KCOW and KXLY was KFPY. Plans called for KXL to feed this Pacific Northwest Broadcasters network (PNB) newscasts and blocks of recorded music. According to the plan, local stations would insert their own commercials and home town information.

While the Z Bar operated into 1957, PNB, later known as the XL Network, did not see many of its programming plans materialize, except for a Saturday afternoon feature known as the "Thousand Mile Quiz." This was an hour (4:30-5:30) program, hosted by a mysterious "Mister XL," who was really Fred Eichorn, a staff announcer at KXL. This weekly quiz was an excellent opportunity for the individual stations to do a little "politicking" and impress the local leaders and businessmen by inviting them to appear on the program. Besides the "Quiz," the eight PNB stations were linked occasionally for special events such as election coverage.

The PNB was a successful sales organization, but it did not live up to expectations as a regional interconnected network. KGCX at Sidney and

KING, Seattle were independently owned affiliates of PNB for a short time in 1946 and 1947.[73]

Other state networks were planned but did not materialize. A. J. Mosby, the Western Montana radio pioneer, envisioned his KGVO as the flagship for the "Art Mosby Stations," a combination of KGVO, KANA at Anaconda and the proposed KGFT at Great Falls. KGVO and KANA were linked occasionally for special programs, but KGFT never got on the air. Another state network, never named, would have been centered around the proposed 5,000 watt KYES at Butte, but the station was not constructed, mainly because there were already four stations in the Butte market.[74]

For a time, because of the method of routing the CBS radio lines, an interconnection of KBOW (Butte), KGVO and KFBB was possible. KBOW could also feed KOOK (Billings). These CBS lines were used on very rare occasions to feed programs between Montana stations, but were not reversible like the interconnections between the Z Bar stations. Once in a while, one of the stations down line would miss taping a network feed and one of the upline stations would feed it to them. At times, this caused problems for the other stations.

In the KGVO control room the amplifier that boosted the incoming CBS signal to KFBB was located in an equipment rack next to a panel, very similar in design, that determined the selection of the audio between the KGVO studio and their transmitter site southwest of town. One studio-transmitter line sent the on-the-air program to the transmitter, while the other was used for various purposes, including a feed of the CBS programs to the transmitter where the engineer on duty took care of the network delay chores. This line could also be used to send a net delay program back to the studio in case local commercials were to be placed within the program as it went out on the air.

On several occasions, a KGVO announcer, intending to change the input of the spare line to the transmitter would instead throw the switch on the CBS-KFBB feed panel, giving the Great Falls station the local KGVO program instead of the network. One afternoon in the fall of 1952 the operator at KFBB joined the network at 3 o'clock for a soap opera, and was greeted by Pat "The Cat" Connell, the afternoon KGVO disc jockey. The KFBB management was enraged by the switching error, especially when listeners began calling, wanting to hear "The Cat" instead of the soap opera. Great Falls was Connell's home town.

The network amplifier was later moved to the local phone company office, out of the reach of the KGVO announcers. Connell, who pronounced his name Caw-nell', went on to become the first person of black descent to be hired by a major network (CBS).[75]

From humble beginnings in 1946, the Intermountain Network (IMN) grew to an interconnection of 23 stations in the Treasure State.[76] The

IMN was also a regional network, covering the entire Rocky Mountain area, plus the Dakotas. For a while, IMN shared satellite service with ABC Radio. It was originally a regional segment of the Mutual Broadcasting System (MBS). Before its demise, IMN had an outlet in nearly every Montana city. This regional network offered many programs that were supplemental to the national network service. They originated at KALL in Salt Lake City, or at KIMN, the affiliate in Denver. Each state maintained its own news bureau, usually in the capital city.

IMN was a boon to small market stations from both a revenue and a programming standpoint. However in recent years, many stations did not carry many of the IMN programs, except for news and farm features. The Montana Intermountain Network was one of the most successful divisions of this regional chain until its demise in the late 1980s.

A connection between KOPR at Butte, KMON in Great Falls and several other ABC stations in Idaho and Utah, known as the Rocky Mountain Broadcasting System (RMBS) existed for a short time in the late 1940s.[77] It was the ABC affiliates' answer to the Intermountain Network. RMBS came to a close when IMN obtained the ABC affiliation in the Mountain West as a supplemental network service. IMN prevailed and RMBS became history. Most former Rocky Mountain stations affiliated with IMN.

Another state hookup, the Northern Ag Network, serves a great number of stations in Montana and Wyoming. NAN is headquartered in Billings and offers farm and ranch information, some weather and uses its lines for state events, such as sports.

In years past, there were a couple of situations where small town operations derived a portion of their daily programming from a station in a larger market. The KXXL (Bozeman) and KWYS (West Yellowstone) hookup was the most active interconnection of this type. KXLL originated all news, sports and weather for the West Yellowstone station. KFLN at Baker also sent programming to KPWD (FM) at Plentywood for a short period of time.

Throughout the years, several sales networks have existed in the state. These combinations did not share programming and were not interconnected. Therefore, they cannot be classified as networks in the classic sense. The "Silver Dollar," "Greater Montana," and "Enterprise" networks are good examples of these sales-oriented combinations. Silver Dollar consisted of KGVO, KXLF, KFBB and KOOK plus a few smaller market stations. Greater Montana was made up of small town outlets such as KRBN at Red Lodge; KHDN, Hardin and KDRG, Deer Lodge. It was also a news-sharing combination, although stations were not interconnected. Enterprize was Christian-oriented stations operated by the CEI Group.

A combination of stations known as the "Bobcat Radio Network (BRN)" has been in operation for several years and exists soley for state-wide coverage of the Montana State University/Bozeman football and basketball games. KBOZ is the flagship for the network. A similar combination, headquartered in Missoula, offers coverage of University of Montana sports and originates with KYLT (AM).

There have been several TV hookups in Montana. "The Montana Television Network (MTN)" was made up of KTVQ, Billings; KXLF-TV in Butte; KRTV at Great Falls and KPAX (TV), Missoula. Eagle Communications, Inc. offers a three station hook-up of KECI (TV), Missoula; KTVM, Butte and KCFW (TV), Kalispell. Other TV stations in the state occasionally linked up with ECI for sports coverage and special events. There was also a short-lived combination of KYUS, Miles City; KOUS, Hardin and KCTZ (TV), Bozeman.

In 1988, a group from Spokane, Washington began operating the Sunbrook Radio Network, a TV sideband interconnection of KGRZ/KDXT, Missoula; KXTL/KQUY, Butte; KXGF/KAAK in Great Falls and KBLG/KRKX, Billings, plus a few independent affiliates.

Montana State University/Billings' KEMC (FM) originates network programming for KECC (FM), Miles City; KBMC (FM), Bozeman and KNMC (FM), Havre, with a repeater planned at Helena. The programs of KUFM at U of M are rebroadcast on KGPR, with repeaters planned for Kalispell, Butte and Hamilton.

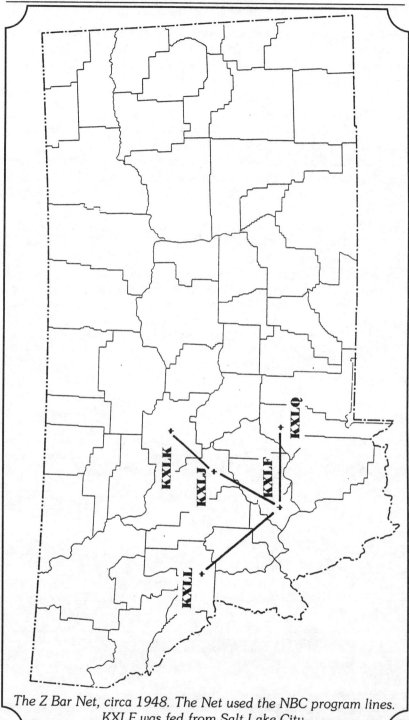

The Z Bar Net, circa 1948. The Net used the NBC program lines.
KXLF was fed from Salt Lake City.

5

Programming

While not always unique, local programming on Montana stations was born of necessity and dictated by need. Early broadcasters such as KDYS, KFBB, KGHL, KGCX and KGIR were forced to rely heavily on local talent, especially musicians.[78] The early program schedules were saturated with live performances, many of which were only semi-professional, or worse. In the pioneer schedules, there was a great amount of time devoted to phonograph records. The recorded selections often detracted from the live performances, because the records were generally more professional.

Gradually, the stations began to schedule regular farm and market reports, weather information and some news, either gathered locally, or read out of the paper. This lead to many variations of programming on the various stations.

One early-day program feature was KFBB's "Farmer's Noon Hour." This was reputed to be the oldest and longest running farm program in the nation, even antedating the WLS "Farm and Home Hour," from Chicago with Everett Mitchell.[79]

The Farmer's Noon Hour began in embryonic form while KFBB was still located in Havre, and expanded once the station relocated to Great Falls. At the height of its popularity, it ran for an hour and a half (12 noon to 1:30 pm) and featured news, market and livestock reports, weather, grain quotations, county extension commentaries and other agri-related information. For years, the familiar strains of the theme song "Yankee Doodle" introduced the program. It was replaced later by a stirring rendition of LeRoy Anderson's "Chicken Reel," complete with crowing roosters and cackling hens.

This package of farm-related information placed a great emphasis on its longevity. A meticulous count of programs was maintained, and each broadcast was individually numbered in the daily introductory remarks. One young KFBB announcer enraged the station management by pream-bling the FNH on one occasion with, "Welcome now to the 'lebendy, 'lebendy, 'lebenth broadcast of the Farmer's Noon Hour."[80]

The FNH was the "sacred cow" of KFBB, and nothing, save a national emergency could pre-empt the program. One former employee maintained, "Only the second coming of Christ could cancel the Noon Hour!"[81]

Other stations had their noon programs, but none outlasted the FNH on KFBB. Even as the various stations affiliated with the national networks, a great emphasis was placed on local programming. In the 1920s and 30s, many stations, especially KFBB and KGCX were happy to transmit personal messages over the airwaves, even though they were technically a violation of FCC rules. The advent of competition after World War II caused many of the old-line stations to drop some of their home-spun and home-town ways and become more "professional." Consequently, many of the older stations lost touch with their listeners of long standing.

Some of the programming on the Z Bar Net was unique. While KGIR contributed the majority of programs to the Z Bar, other stations began to augment the network schedule as the years passed. KRBM in cooperation with the Agricultural Extension Service at Montana State College in Bozeman, produced a weekly "Farm Journal of the Air," Saturday mornings at seven o'clock. At Helena, KPFA[82] originated several daily Z Bar newscasts. The Helena station was in the unique position of having the offices of United Press on the second floor of their studio-office building.[83] KXLJ also fed a daily children's show to the network for several years.

The Missoula affiliate, KXLL, produced a weekly musical entity known as "The Highlander Tavern," a simulated broadcast from a mythical nightspot at an unknown location, sponsored by a local brewery. The host announcer would play recorded crowd noise under his patter and pretend to talk to the patrons and bartender. Music consisted of polkas and other "oompah-type" renditions. The program was started by one of the area's favorite announcers, Bill Strothman. The host who officiated at the "Tavern" for the longest period of time was Robert "Bob" Lasich, a Butte native who became a prominent newscaster in the San Francisco area on NBC's KNBR.

A tourist-oriented program, "The Montana Boosters," ran for many years on Z Bar, and was hosted by KXLF manager Arnie Anzjon, with other stations contributing tourist information and similar data to the program. Anzjon opened the festivities each weekday afternoon with the recorded bellowing of a male bovine who became known as "Elmer the Z Bar Bull."[84]

In the 1940s, KGVO at Missoula broadcast a three-times-a-week remote in front of the Florence Hotel in downtown Missoula. This was a typical "Man on the Street" broadcast, hosted by staff announcer W. C. "Bud" Blanchette. At the age of thirteen, the author made his radio debut on the program and was allowed to read a commercial for a local dairy.

Montana was represented in the stable of "soap operas" that occupied a major portion of the daily broadcast schedule on three of the four major networks. For several years, ABC originated a serial known as "Lone Journey," written by Montanan Paul "Gunnar" Mickelson. This radio drama was set in Central Montana, around the city of Lewistown. The scripts often made mention of local places and landmarks such as the Rainbow Hotel in Great Falls, Square Butte and the various mountain ranges of Montana's heartland.

The main characters, Nita and Wolfe Bennett, were "typical" Montana people who owned the Spear-T cattle ranch. The Bennetts had many relatives in the East and nearby Montana towns. Occasionally, actual residents of the area were mentioned on the air. "Lone Journey" was heard on ABC (Blue) each weekday morning at 10:15 MST.

Mickelson's sister, Sandra Michael, was the originator and for years chief writer for another drama, "Against the Storm," which had a west coast setting. Both radio "soaps" drew a large audience on state ABC affiliates because of their local connection, especially on KMON and KXLO. "Against the Storm" had a short-lived run on ABC-TV.

Network programming, or the lack of it, often had an effect on the fare offered by Montana stations. After World War II, most stations took on affiliation with one of the major networks (NBC, CBS, ABC or Mutual). Often, it was only a partial affiliation, especially in the days between 1935 and 1941. Many network advertisers were reluctant to buy the entire hookup, especially the remote areas of the West where their products were not marketed. Most of the major networks also sold advertising on a regional basis, often leaving the West out entirely, except for major cities on the Pacific coast.

Both NBC and CBS had an afternoon "block" of dramas or "soaps" that occupied the time from noon to 4 pm, Mountain time. In many cases, only a few of these programs were ordered for the mountain zone. This left many "holes" or spaces in the afternoon that western stations had to fill locally.

Usually, either a locally originated musical program or a syndicated soap opera was used to fill the space in the schedule. KGIR sold these programs to local grocery stores that offered the items advertised on the network soap operas. KGHL had a hole at 1:45 in the afternoon that was used to program farm and market reports. In at least one instance, the Z Bar Net did not even attempt to secure an NBC program that could have been ordered for their station. "Hymns of All Churches," a part of NBC's "General Mills Hour," which ran from noon to 1 pm MST, did not begin to offer the compensation the net could obtain from a Z Bar origi- nated news program sponsored by Texaco at 12:45 daily.

A syndicated cooking program, "Mary Lee Taylor," was heard on the Z Bar Net, KFBB and several other stations in the state. It was sponsored by a flour milling company, and featured Mary Lee and her helper, Benny Walker, as they fussed around the studio, giving recipes for the daily kitchen concoction, which always came out of Mary Lee's oven just exactly right.

Montana CBS stations had a problem in the morning hours when they were not ordered for many of the CBS soaps. KGVO and KFBB attempted for many years to delay the CBS dramas from early in the morning into a block later in the day, but the recordings were not acceptable, either to the network or the listener. The stations used cheap acetate recording discs for the delay and the quality was close to horrible.

After the soap operas ceased to be sponsored by a single advertiser, stations sometimes "covered" network commercials within the program if they were not ordered for that particular station. Some operators, like Art Mosby of KGVO and the management of KFBB even refused to carry a "soap" if it ran for several days without a sponsor, leaving some very dismayed and angry listeners.

In general, evening programs from the networks were not a problem because most advertisers were inclined to buy the whole network, although there were exceptions. For many years, NBC programmed an entire Monday evening of music, offering such programs as "The Voice of Firestone," "The Bell Telephone Hour," "The Railroad Hour" and "The Cavalcade of America." These were either classical or show music programs, performed live in New York or Hollywood. One NBC Monday night offering, "The Band of America," with Paul Lavalle, was sponsored by the Cities Service Oil Company, which did not have stations in the West. Many NBC stations were required to offer local programming instead of the "Band." KRBM (KXLQ) at Bozeman continued the classical music fare with a program hosted by station manager Ernest "Ernie" Neath who was an accomplished musician.

CBS stations had a smiliar difficulty on Friday nights with a network mystery program, "The Whistler." The show was fed to Pacific and Mountain stations under the sponsorship of the Signal Oil Company. Signal did not have stations in Montana and parts of the Northwest. At Missoula, KGVO filled the void by offering a live country music program, "The Johnny Ziesmer Show," performed before a studio audience. The program showcased the talents of a four-piece band for 15 minutes each week, and was hosted by Bud Blanchette who introduced the songs and generally gave the "boys in the band" a hard time. The remaining quarter hour was filled by Marion Dixon, the station manager, who read poetry over recorded piano and organ music. CBS also offered "Vox Pop," an opinion-news program that had an eastern sponsor and was not heard in Montana.

In the final days of NBC's "Fibber Magee and Molly," Johnson's Wax, their mentors for many years, dropped sponsorship of the program. It was picked up by the Pet Milk Company, which did not market its product in the Mountain Zone. A subsidiary, Sego Milk of Utah, sponsored the show in the mountains. The program was delayed one week by KDYL in Salt Lake City where the Sego commercials were inserted into the program.

Montana stations also relied heavily on syndicated radio programs, produced by both independent studios and subsidiaries of the major networks. These programs were shipped to the stations on high quality acetate discs. Provision was made for places at the beginning, end and within the program for local and regional sponsor identification and their commercials.

In the years before either ABC (The Blue Network) or Mutual had affiliates in Montana, some of the programs were syndicated to stations within the state. "Lum 'n Abner," a popular rural comedy program, was heard in Montana on a six week delay through the Keystone Broadcasting System (KBS), a non-interconnected network that relied on disc recordings. Lum 'n Abner was sponsored by Alka-Seltzer in Montana on the Z Bar Net and KGEZ. "The Lone Ranger" and "Green Hornet" programs were also syndicated and offered in Montana on disc through Mutual and the originating station, WXYZ in Detroit.

For several years, KGIR filled a hole in the afternoon soap opera schedule with a syndicated feature known as "The Knights of the Road," which starred two characters who were a composite of Amos 'n' Andy, Lum 'n' Abner and Pete the Tramp of the comic strips. The program was sponsored by a Butte Bakery. KGIR also broadcast the syndicated series, "Cub Reporter." KRBM at Bozeman offered young listeners two programs, "Secret City," and "The Adventures of Hop Harrigan," the story of a World War II Navy pilot. Both were programmed in the afternoon when school was out for the day.

A Hollywood firm known as C. P. MacGregor Productions had quite a stable of programs on disc that were heard through Montana. The show, "C. P. MacGregor Presents," featured the producer himself in a program that was very similar to the CBS production, "The Lux Radio Theatre." Ed Craney at KGIR was the Montana distributor for the MacGregor programs, and made enough by selling the programs to other stations in the state to pay his own fees to the producer.

MacGregor offered a couple of mystery programs and musical shows, including "The Sons of the Pioneers," during days when the group included "Foghorn" Farr and a singer named Leonard Slye, who later became known as Roy Rogers. KGVO was still running "Sons of the Pioneers" in their noon hour as late as 1963. Somewhere along the line, KRBN at

Red Lodge acquired the complete syndicated series, "Jerry of the Circus," and the sequel, "Jerry at Fair Oaks." These programs were broadcast on a "bootleg" basis for the first two years of the station's operation.

RCA/NBC was the source of the Thesaurus Library, which offered music on disc, sales aids, commercial jingles, sound effects and a variety of half-hour programs such as the "Weird Circle," and the "Haunting Hour," two offerings that bore a strange resemblance to the CBS "Inner Sanctum" series.

Ziv Radio Productions, which later ventured into the field of TV syndication, offered a variety of off-network shows, both in the musical and dramatic categories. One of the most popular, especially in the years after World War II, was a radio adaptation of Matt Svetic's, "I Was a Communist for the FBI." Montana stations relied heavily on Ziv productions.

Lang-Worth Recordings, a music service that offered various styles of music on 33⅓ discs, also offered recorded programs, along with a script service that supposedly allowed the stations to showcase the Lang-Worth music as it might have been presented in a major market, using the LW scripts and local announcers. It never worked out that way. Most of the scripts were poorly written, and few stations used that part of the service.

When KBMN at Bozeman came on the air in 1949, they had no network affiliation. They looked to Ziv, MacGreagor, the Associated library and other syndicators for their nighttime programming that was in competition with the NBC Radio evening line-up of KXLQ, across town.

Following World War II, The United States went off "War Time," which was the same as today's daylight saving time, except it was in effect year around. The following summer (1946) many of the states adopted Daylight time, but most of the Western states, including Montana, declined to go along with the advanced time. This left Montana radio stations in a quandary, because all network programs came to them one hour earlier than normal.

This meant a soap opera such as the "Road of Life," moved from its 8:30 am hour to 7:30, a time usually reserved for polka music and market reports. In the evening, all the top flight network programs were heard an hour earlier, placing shows like the "Voice of Firestone," at 5:30 instead of the usual 6:30 "after supper" time. This played havoc with the stations' local newscast schedule and other local programming. For a few years, Butte and Anaconda, because of pressure from the labor unions, went on Daylight time, while the rest of the state remained on standard reckoning. Confusion turned to chaos as stations in Butte and Anaconda were forced to give all time checks in both Daylight and standard terms. Farm folks, and others in rural areas left home in the middle of the afternoon to shop and conduct business in Butte, only to find the stores and offices closed when they got there because of the advanced time.

Eventually, the networks began delaying all their programs one hour and supplying them to standard time stations on a special network. This resulted in an FCC ruling that required standard stations to make what became known as the "summer-all" announcement:

> "Because of Daylight Saving Time in parts of the nation, some or all of the network programs broadcast on this station are delayed one hour by means of transcription."

For several years, KGHL at Billings held the contract from NBC to provide the tape delay for a portion of the West.

When Daylight Time became the norm for most of the nation, the four networks had gone to a "news on the hour" and features program format that did not require the one hour delay.

Looking back, as radio broadcasting began in Montana, the "formats" or program plans were very similar at most stations. They broadcast a variety of news, usually read out of the paper (or from a press service) along with market summaries, weather reports and a variety of music. Recordings were usually whatever the station owned or could borrow from stores or listeners.

With the advent of the 1930s and 40s, much programming came from the national networks, with soap operas prevailing in the morning hours and early afternoon. Variety, music and comedy shows made up the bulk of the evening schedules. Time between network programs was filled with music and locally oriented news and features, such as women's programs. Many stations offered Country-Western music in the early morning, with current popular music in the afternoon. Stations either broadcast late-night dance orchestras from their networks or offered recorded easy-listening orchestras and vocals in the last hours of their broadcast day.

By the mid 1950s, the radio networks declined and stations looked more and more to music and news as programming options. The first Montana station to be programmed along a particular format or music form was KRBN at Red Lodge which billed itself as "Montana's Only Fulltime Country-Western Station."

At the same time, many Montana stations followed the popular trend toward Gordon McLendon/Todd Storz radio formats that placed a great emphasis on rock and roll music and personality disc jockeys. Although many Montana stations broadcast this format, few did it successfully. Others looked to Country music or "easy-listening" as their niche in the market.

The FM stations pioneered by Christian Enterprises, KGVW-FM, Belgrade; KURL-FM, Billings and KIVE (FM), Glendive were the first to offer fulltime easy listening formats.

By the late 1960s and 70s, nearly every station in the state had selected a definite format. Most markets boasted at least one Country, Contemporary Hit or "Oldies" outlet along with a "beautiful music" station.

When talk radio began in the 1980s at KBLG in Billings, other stations followed, especially after the advent of such talk and controversy radio hosts as Rush Limbaugh, G. Gordon Liddy, Bruce Williams and Michael Reagan.

6

Broadcast Equipment And Engineering

When KDYS and KFBB began in Montana in the 1920s, there were few commercially manufactured radio transmitters or other broadcast gear on the market. Most stations would not have been able to afford the equipment if it had been available. Therefore, nearly all broadcasting gear was home-made.

KDYS's first transmitter was a home-brew affair, consisting of two 50 watt tubes, and was assembled by C. W. Wilks of Great Falls.[85] Likewise, F. A. Buttrey began KFBB with a 50 watt home-constructed transmitter connected to a "flat top" antenna that was located on the roof of his department store in downtown Havre.[86] Following the move to Great Falls in 1929, KFBB was upgraded continually and in 1939 the station installed a new Western Electric 5 Kw transmitter that utilized an "inverse feedback" circuit to improve the broadcast signal.[87] This water-cooled unit was in service continuously until an early morning fire destroyed the KFBB Radio-TV Center west of Great Falls in 1967.

In the early 1960s, the old KFBB transmitter was quite a curiosity. Modern day engineers considered it a wonderful relic and antique and would travel hundreds of miles just to view the old unit in operation. KFBB also utilized a variety of custom-made units, both in their radio and TV studios. KFBB's engineering team, Tony Lopuch and Wilbur Myhre, built and installed one of the nations first automatic "limiters" in the station's circuitry, long before the commercial units became popular. A limiter prevents a radio station from overmodulating.

At Butte, KGIR moved its studios and transmitter to Nissler Junction west of town in 1937 and increased power to 5,000 watts.[88] The old 1,000 watt transmitter that had been used in the former downtown location was retired. The need for a new transmitter resulted in one of the best "composite" or custom-made transmitters ever assembled for a broadcast station. Not only was the work of engineer Jack Provis an electronic masterpiece, the wood and glass cabinetry that housed the electrical components were a cabinetmaker's delight. This transmitter served KGIR/ KXLF well into the 1960s.

Provis, who was also corporate engineer for the Z Bar Net, built a set of customized audio consoles for the five stations that allowed easy switching of program material between the affiliates.

At KGHL, long-time engineer Fred "Fritz" Bartlett and his predecessor, Jeff Kiichli, constructed a variety of equipment that kept the station "sounding like a million" for years. Many engineers at the other Montana stations performed small miracles when it came to building their own equipment and keeping the stations on the air, oftimes on a limited engineering budget. Unfortunately, managers who were not familiar with the many facets of broadcast electronics, failed to have real appreciation for their engineers, and thought of them as leading candidates for the office of Village Idiot. Many talented engineers went unappreciated and under paid.

Most pioneer Montana stations maintained what was known as a "split operation," whereby the studios and offices were located downtown and the transmitter was somewhere outside the city. This was long before the FCC authorized remote control operation, and it was necessary to have both an announcer at the studio and an operator, or engineer, at the transmitter. Several stations used the transmitter operator to accomplish tape delays of network programs, thus freeing the announcer for other chores, such as answering the phone, writing commercial "copy" or studio cleanup. In the years before commercial tape recorders, the engineer at the transmitter often recorded network programs on acetate discs for later broadcast.

Many stations had a small studio at the transmitter site where the programming could originate in case of an emergency. At KFBB, in the days before television, the transmitter operator made the station breaks after ten o'clock in the evening so the uptown studio could close for the night.

In Montana, KGVO, KGHL, KFBB and KGCX used this type of operation for years until remote control was authorized. At Kalispell, KGEZ maintained a unique arrangement, with the announcer in town, seated before a microphone in the studio-office suite, and the engineer at the transmitter playing phonograph records and transcriptions that made up the broadcast day.

The Z Bar Net stations were strictly "combo-operations" with the studios and transmitter in the same building. This required all announcers to also be licensed engineers. In the early days, and even into the late 1950s, all operators were required to hold an FCC First Class Radio-telephone license. Strangely, the pay scale for the "combo-men" was seldom any higher than the announcers and engineers at stations that were "split." A majority of the new stations that began following World War II were combo operations, except for KMON at Great Falls and KOPR, Butte.

7

Station Ownership

All of Montana's pioneer (pre World War II) radio stations were locally owned and mostly financed by Montana money. Innovators like F. A. Buttrey, the Great Falls Tribune, Ed Craney, Ed Krebsbach, Charles Campbell and Art Mosby had other interests that helped provide the capital for their radio endeavors.

Buttrey owned a department store, Campbell an auto supply company and Mosby an electrical shop. Craney and Krebsbach obtained financing from associates.[89] Craney took on a variety of partners to build the Z Bar Net, including Montana politician Barclay Craighead.

Following World War II, the situation changed only slightly, the original KOPR at Butte being a possible exception. The Butte station claimed to be "financed by prominent Butte and Salt Lake businessmen," but most of the dignitaries on hand at the station's opening ceremonies were from out of town.[90] The station was later purchased by George Hatch and associates of Salt Lake City, merged with KBOW and today is mostly owned by Montana investors.

Many post-war stations such as KANA, KXLL and KXLK were constructed by established Montana broadcasters. Some were built by sales people and announcers who had been employed by other Montana stations. Very little out-of-state ownership occurred until after the Korean War era when several "foreign" interests either built or purchased stations in the Treasure State. KQDI (formerly KBGF) at Great Falls, KYYA (Y-93) in Billings and KERR, Polson are examples of out-of-state interests that purchased or built stations in Montana.

Although it was not an attempted acquisition of a Montana station by out-of-state interests, the proposed purchase of KFBB by the Fairmont Corporation stimulated a rash of controversy in the state.

In January 1951, Fred Birch, a Great Falls contractor and owner of KFBB, petitioned the FCC to authorize the transfer of majority ownership of the station (51%) to Fairmont. The request would probably have gone unnoticed by the general public, except for the fact that Fairmont was a subsidiary of the giant Anaconda Copper (ACM) interests. Anaconda at that time held the major newspapers in Butte, Missoula, Helena, Billings, Livingston and several smaller communities.

The purchase was seen by labor groups, farm organizations and many others as an attempt by ACM to extend its influence into the Great Falls market where they did not own a newspaper. The FCC was deluged with letters and petitions of protest. Some of the correspondence bypassed the agency and was submitted directly to President Truman and Montana Senator James Murray.

In February of 1952, Fairmont quietly requested that the FCC dismiss the application for transfer of ownership.[91]

In recent years, and in addition to those interests already mentioned, the prime manifestation of out-of-state ownership has been the Spokane based Sunbrook Communications Group (see section on networks), operating stations in Missoula, Butte, Great Falls and Billings.

Out-of-staters have also purchased a controlling interest in the Montana Television Network (MTN) stations in Butte, Great Falls, Missoula and Billings.

8

Out Of State Signals

While the stations that developed in Montana prior to World War II were practically without competition in their individual markets during the daytime, signals from a variety of clear channel stations penetrated the state after sundown, giving the listener a variety of programs to choose from. By 1940, most of the stations in the Treasure State were operating with powers of either 5,000 or 250 watts during the daytime and utilized either reduced power or directional antennas at night. The one exception was KGIR (KXLF) which was unique in being able to operate with 5,000 watts, day and night, non-directional.

Many areas in the state were left without dependable local service at night. Even in cities such as Great Falls, Billings and Butte, radio listeners often chose programs from afar that were not available on the local station.

In radio's early days, "DXing," or distance reception, was a favorite evening pastime and Montanans were not immune. Many of the great clear channel stations boomed into Montana at night, especially during the winter months when the temperature hovered near the zero mark. Great 50,000 watt outlets such as KGO and KPO, San Francisco, KNX and KFI, Los Angeles; KOB, Albuquerque; KSL, Salt Lake City and KOA in Denver were common evening fare in many Montana city homes and rural homesteads.

The fun began soon after sundown with the great giants of the Midwest, such as WHO, Des Moines; KFAB at Omaha; WLS, WBBM and WGN in Chicago; along with WCCO, Minneapolis and WWL, New Orleans came crackling through home radio speakers. Then, the west coast giants would begin to come in, along with the super-power stations in Mexico, such as XERB, Rosario Beach, Baja California and XELO, Juarez, mailing address: Clint, Texas! It was a nighttime radio wonderland and a difficult act for the Montana stations to follow. On cold winter evenings, especially during clear weather, it was often possible to thrill to the sound of WEAF, New York; WSM at Nashville (you could hear the "Grand Ole Opry" live and direct); WBZ in Boston and KDKA, Pittsburgh. During the time when WLW in Cincinnati was operating experimentally with 500,000 watts, they could be heard in Montana in the daytime during the winter. The only time Montana stations were without serious out-of-state competition in the evening was during mid-summer when the clears did not begin to skip into the state until 9:30 or 10 o'clock in the evening.

In the years before World War II, neither the Mutual Broadcasting System (MBS) nor the NBC Blue Network (later on A-B-C), had affiliates in Montana except for special hookups and programs delayed by transcription. Montana listeners relied on out-of-state MBS and Blue stations to give them a listening alternative to the NBC and CBS fare offered by state network affiliates. During the fall and winter months KLO at Ogden, Utah placed a good late afternoon and evening signal into many sections of Southern Montana, allowing listeners to hear Mutual programs. KGO in San Francisco was a good nighttime source for Blue Network offerings as was KEX, Portland.

Montanans were fortunate in being able to enjoy programming from the Canadian Broadcasting Corporation (CBC) through CFCN at Calgary, Alberta and CBK, Watrous, Saskatchewan.

9

Music Licensing

When radio began, both in Montana and the United States, a great amount of recorded music was used on the air. At first, music publishers and the record companies encouraged the use of their wares on the radio. It gave listeners a sample of what was being produced, and in their minds, stimulated and promoted record sales. As broadcasting became a commercial medium, and stations began to obtain income from the sale of advertising, the same record companies and publishers began to seek compensation for the use of their music.

The American Society of Composers, Authors and Publishers (ASCAP), was formed in 1914 to protect the rights of the music industry. In the 1920s, ASCAP began to agitate for royalties from the broadcasters in return for the use of their music on the air. At that time, ASCAP controlled practically all music except for a few selections that were considered in the public domain (PD). As ASCAP became more demanding, various stations and other related interests formed the National Association of Broadcasters (NAB), mainly as a common front against ASCAP.

By 1930, ASCAP was collecting $800,000 or 40 percent of its income from radio performance fees. A continual battle raged between ASCAP and the NAB because ASCAP believed the use of copyright music on the air was harming sheet music sales and the record business. By 1939, broadcasters established a fund to create a new music licensing agency, owned by broadcasters. The new venture, known as Broadcast Music, Inc. (BMI), was set afloat with the idea of building their own music library, in competition with ASCAP and to offer lower licensing rates.[92]

When most radio stations refused to renew their ASCAP contracts at the beginning of 1941, listeners were subjected to a very limited list of BMI and a variety of music that was in the public domain, such as "Jeanie With the Light Brown Hair."[93]

Several Montana broadcasters, notably Ed Craney (Z Bar Net) and Art Mosby (KGVO) as well as a few others, determined to fight ASCAP to the finish. It was not until both owners had completely divested themselves of their broadcast properties that they were finally covered under blanket licenses and could play music at their leisure from either ASCAP or BMI.[94]

Craney, Mosby and others such as Fred Birch, who had purchased KFBB from F. A. Buttrey, held BMI blanket licenses, but had only "per-performance" arrangements with ASCAP. This meant the stations paid a fee to ASCAP for each record they aired, and it was necessary to keep a listing, or music log, of all records played, for the benefit of ASCAP. Therefore, the local announcer had not only his program log, and in some cases a transmitter log to maintain, but a music log as well.

In the days when the stations broadcast a great number of network programs, the music log was nothing more than a nuisance, but as the years went by, and more and more local programming was offered, mainly in the form of disc jockey programs, the logging of music became an almost unsurmountable task for the announcers. All music had to be logged, even BMI material that was covered by the blanket license, for the benefit of ASCAP. Some operators, like Craney, allowed ASCAP music to be used only on sponsored programs in order that the music fee could be passed on to the advertisers.

In 1951, the author hosted a late-night DJ show on KXLQ in Bozeman. This was a request program known as "Sandman Serenade." Listeners called in requests for various musical selections, mainly the current hit songs. Because of the licensing problem, the DJ was required to play a 15 minute block of ASCAP music and then a quarter hour segment of BMI material. Due to this limitation, listeners were often required to wait up to half an hour for their requests.[95]

Because the manager felt the disc jockey was becoming "too popular," the program was discontinued in favor of the late-evening NBC network dance orchestra broadcasts. Cross-town competitor KBMN immediately began a call-in request program at the same evening hour. KBMN had a blanket license with both ASCAP and BMI.[96]

Today all Montana stations have blanket license agreements with AS-CAP and BMI, as well as a small music firm known as SESAC. SESAC has the performance rights to just enough music to be a thorn in the side of broadcasters. Their representatives have been known to sit in a local motel room for days with a receiver and tape recorder, waiting for some unsuspecting station without a SESAC license to play one of their songs. The representative then offers the station manager the choice of a law suit or signing a SESAC license. In all fairness to SESAC, their music repertory is increasing, especially in the field of country music.

More material on the Music Licensing Battle can be found in the section entitled, "There Was a Fellow by the Name of Craney."

10

FM & Television

Frequency Modulation (FM) broadcasting, like educational TV, had a slow start in Montana. It was the last state in the Union to be granted a construction permit for an FM station. The pioneer FM facility was not in one of the state's larger cities, but in the small village of Plentywood. KPWD (FM) began broadcasting on June 1, 1962. Others were slow to follow because of the lack of FM receivers.

The Enterprise Network, a group of Christian-oriented stations, built the second and third stations in the state, with KGVW-FM going on the air at Belgrade on November 1, 1963 and KURL-FM in Billings commencing six weeks later on December 17th. At Great Falls, KARR-FM opened for business on New Year's Eve of the same year. The state's first FM educational station, KUFM, started at the University of Montana campus in Missoula on January 31, 1965.[97]

Bozeman almost had an FM station in 1966. An employee of KGVW at Belgrade decided to build his own station in Bozeman. Ben Hespen had obtained a construction permit, was assigned call letters and had partially erected a building to house the station. Hespen was a teacher, had an employment opportunity in Havre, and the project was cancelled for lack of interest. Hespen's call sign, KBFM, was later assigned to an FM station in Denver.[98]

FM experienced a phenomenal growth during the 1970s and 80s. Today, there are 60 FM stations in Montana. Nine of them are educational, and others, both commercial and educational are being planned.

As in many cities around the nation, FM began in Montana featuring "Beautiful Music" formats on stations such as KGVW-FM at Belgrade; KURL-FM in Billings and Butte's KBOW-FM. In recent years, the FM band has been taken over by stations with modern formats such as Contemporary Hit Radio (CHR), Country Music (CW) and a variety of "Oldies" formats.

One result of the rapid growth of FM in Montana has been several "FM only" cities and towns where the primary or only radio service is FM.

At present, Chinook, Ronan, Malta and Scobey are served only by FM stations with AM available from out-lying areas.

Several Montana markets are monopolistic situations, where both the city's AM and FM stations are under common ownership. This scenario exists at Dillon, Forsyth, Glasgow, Sidney, Hamilton, Lewistown, Libby, Shelby, Plentywood, Polson-Ronan and Wolf Point.

FM translators have been a great assist in developing the medium in Montana, allowing stations to expand their coverage areas and revenue bases. A translator is a low-power repeater station that operates on an unused channel apart from the station it "translates." These translators cannot originate local programming and are limited in their power output.

Translators are used in remote areas such as Big Sky and Colstrip to bring FM service from larger cities. Montana State University/Billings (through KEMC) has used an intricate network of translators to place their signal into many Wyoming and Montana communities where they would not otherwise be heard. MSU/Billings has also built a 50,000 watt FM near Bozeman (KBMC) that relays KEMC programming and has replaced some of its translators.[99]

Translators are also utilized by commercial FM stations to increase their coverage areas.

Television, like FM, began late in Montana. The huge expense that came with the construction of a new facility, along with the long standing FCC "freeze" imposed on new TV station construction in the early 1950s, kept the medium out of the state until 1953.

Interest in TV antedated the first Television station by several years. A few electronic buffs dreamed of locating huge, high gain antennas atop mountain tops in order to receive stations from Salt Lake City, Denver and Spokane. Some of these installations were actually built, and worked, bringing in "skip" reception from a variety of distant cities. One video devotee, with a huge antenna located on one of the highest points in the city of Butte, was watching a station in Salt Lake City on a regular basis early in 1950.

Montana's Z Bar Net pioneer Ed Craney was responsible for the state's first TV station. KXLF-TV at Butte began broadcasting on August 14, 1953 with several hours of evening programming to a handful of local sets.[100]

Craney had a captive market for only 14 days. Butte's second TV station, KOPR-TV, followed, signing on two weeks later on August 28, and made Butte the smallest city in the country with two TV stations. The ensuing battle between the two was fierce, with both sides promising a fight to the finish!

First of all, Craney offered Butte area merchants free KXLF radio time as a bonus if they purchased advertising on his TV station. The management of KOPR refused to follow his lead, and Craney scored round one in a battle that was to last a year.

Several of KOPR's employees had worked for Craney at one time and he used his knowledge of their shortcomings to win the "Battle of Butte TV" once and for all.

Tom Jenkins, KXLF's corporate engineer during this time, was an eye witness to this struggle for survival. In Jenkins' estimation, Craney scored a severe blow which not only helped bring on the close of KOPR's TV station, but probably hastened the demise of their radio outlet a few years later.

Craney started a rumor that his station was talking with Ziv-TV, a film distributor, about purchasing their entire library of films and would be offering them to Butte area advertisers and viewers during the daytime hours, times when neither station had been operating prior to that time. When word of the "impending buy" reached the ears of the KOPR film buyer, he contacted Ziv Productions and signed a contract for their entire stable of films, with no commitment on the part of any local or national sponsor.

The purchase not only pushed KOPR's resources to the limit, but after the papers were signed, the station found no Butte area sponsor was willing to venture into daytime Television, or pledge themselves to programs that were mostly unknown and not running on the major networks.

KOPR was left holding the bag (of films) with no source of income to offset the huge purchase from Ziv. The film buyer was fired, but that did nothing to ease the pain in KOPR's pocketbook. The event started a downhill slide KOPR was unable to overcome. It caused the station to "go dark" just one year and two weeks after it began broadcasting.

This left KXLF-TV alone in the market, ready to pick up viewers, a few sponsors and KOPR's network.

Later, KXLF-TV moved onto channel four, which had been occupied by KOPR. No one ventured into the Butte TV market again until 1970, after Craney had sold the station and left town.

KXLF-TV was not without innovative programming for the Butte area. One of the first locally produced TV shows was an afternoon children's program known as "Kixlif the Klown,"[101] patterned after "Bozo" of network television fame. One of the station's first regular news shows was hosted by announcer George Oschli, who had the ability to memorize his entire newscast. Oschli would deliver the news, seated on the edge of his desk, without assistance from notes or teleprompter.

Both 1953 and '54 were banner years for new TV stations in Montana. Besides the stations at Butte, KOOK-TV began at Billings on November 9, 1953 with their new transmitter building overlooking the city from the eastern rimrocks. Art Mosby began KGVO-TV at Missoula on July first of 1954, following the advent of KFBB-TV at Great Falls on March 21.

Meanwhile, Ed Craney of KXLF, who was responsible for the state's first radio network, began planning the state's first TV network. Craney put KXLJ-TV in Helena on the air January 7, 1958 and immediately made the station a satellite of his Butte outlet. KXLJ-TV originated only a few local spot announcements and an occasional public service program.[102]

In 1959, Craney pioneered the Skyline Television Network. This was a series of off-the-air pickups that consisted of KLIX-TV at Twin Falls, Idaho; KID-TV at Idaho Falls, the stations at Butte and Helena along with KFBB-TV at Great Falls. Because the individual stations supposedly could not afford regular telephone company microwave interconnections to the major networks, an off-the-air pickup was used. The Twin Falls station picked up signals from Salt Lake City and rebroadcast them. In turn, their signal was retransmitted by the station at Idaho Falls. The process was repeated upline until the programming reached Great Falls. The resulting picture and audio quality was inferior to say the least and many viewers petitioned the stations to return to films or interconnect directly with the network.

At Great Falls, when the 1959 World Series games failed to materialize on Skyline, one of the AM stations in town (KUDI) broadcast an inning-by-inning summary, tagged with the comment, "You didn't see it live on Channel Five," an obvious reference to KFBB-TV. This enraged the KFBB management, but nothing ever came of it!

The late 1950s and early 1960s were the heydays for the illegal TV translator. While the FCC hesitated to authorize translators on the UHF band and refused to even consider VHF operation, clandestine repeaters of all sorts flourished in Montana. Practically every town that was within a fringe area of one of the state's TV stations had some sort of translator, usually jury-rigged by a local TV repairman or other electronic buff. Ed Craney worked hard to persuade the FCC to legalize these translators, while at the same time he fought the cable (CATV) systems tooth and toenail, believing their importation of out-of-state signals would spell disaster for Montana TV stations.

An FCC commissioner visited Montana, and returned to Washington, D.C. to report he suspected there was an illegal translator behind every hill and butte in Montana. The FCC finally capitulated and authorized both UHF and VHF operation for translators, as well as cable TV limits.

Two of Montana's television stations were truly unique. Dan Snyder and his associates began KRTV at Great Falls on October 5, 1958. They had purchased a construction permit from Cascade Broadcasters, an out-of-state company that decided not to build a station in the Great Falls Market. KMON had let a permit for Channel Three lapse in the early '50s.

The station began on the proverbial shoestring. An old steel and concrete "quonset" type building, located on a hill north of town was purchased. A 50 foot tower was erected to hold the station's antenna and a variety of used and mostly obsolete equipment was purchased and installed in the building.

KRTV (channel three) went on the air with no network affiliation and programmed syndicated material that had not been seen in the Great Falls market.

Although the station operated with only a few hundred watts and barely covered the city, it was an instant success. It was also a study in informality, and in the eyes of some, unprofessionalism. Snyder and his fellow workers sold advertising during the day and ran the station at night. They had become well known in the area through a previous affiliation with KBGF, a local radio station. Snyder and Ed Kohlman would spend long periods of time clowning around before the station's single camera, either doing a commercial, or filling time if a projector had failed, or other technical problems developed.

Saturdays at KRTV were highlighted by a late night program known as the "World's Worst Movies." Snyder and one of his other staffers spent more time on camera panning the feature film and otherwise horsing around than they did showing the movie. Viewers loved it! The more across-town KFBB-TV panned the new station, the more people watched it.

A late Friday night spot was reserved for horror films and was hosted by a Dracula-like character known as Count Atroa (aorta spelled backward). The "Count" was an anonymous airman from nearby Malmstron Air Force Base who had previous TV experience.

Anything could happen on KRTV. People walked on and off the camera in the middle of commercials and newscasts. At times, it seemed to be nothing more than organized confusion, but viewers and sponsors came back for more! It was their station. Snyder and his associates eventually sold KRTV to the Montana Television Network. It became "just another TV station."

Likewise, KYUS (Cayuse) TV at Miles City was a study in informality and the ultimate small town TV station. Dave and Ella Rivenes began the operation on August 29, 1969 with the help of three student "engineers." The station acquired NBC-TV affiliation, but the 13 hours of network did not pay its own way, so it was up to Rivenes and company to produce two and one-half hours of local programming that paid the bills.

Dave and Ella wrote their own news, produced their own commercials, acted as their own salesmen and attracted an extremely loyal audience.

Most of the time, only one person was on hand to operate the station. Dave Rivenes, or another operator would turn on the camera in the studio for a commercial or newscast and then wander into camera range and sit at the table or desk. When the announcement or newscast was over, he would get up and return to the operating console and place the next event on the air, leaving viewers to watch an empty chair or table. Dave Rivenes delivered many a newscast from his desk with his pet cat asleep alongside his newscopy on the desk top. The viewers ate it up. Rivenes even had an occasion to do an "on the spot" broadcast of a small flood that came through the KYUS studio.[103]

KYUS was a vital part of the Miles City community for many years. In 1985 it became a satellite to KOUS at Hardin and "the old ways were no more."

Every TV station operating in Montana today had a multitude of initial problems, but channel 13 at Missoula probably inherited more than their share. Maybe it was the channel number that brought on the bad luck, or perhaps it was simply a case of the station being in the wrong situation at the wrong time. In any event, "wrong" was the byword at "Lucky-13" for several of their early years.

Broadcast pioneer A.J. "Art" Mosby decided to build a TV companion for his KGVO and chose channel 13. Television channel eight was also assigned to Missoula, but there were several applications for that facility, and no one had sought the higher channel. Mosby applied for it and received a construction permit while the other applicants were still going through the competitive hearings at the FCC.

Preliminary studies by the Mosby engineers indicated the new KGVO-TV could not begin to cover the Missoula trade area if the transmitter and tower were located in town. Height was critical if the station were to place a signal into Hamilton and Polson. Mosby secured Forest Service approval to construct a tower and transmitter-studio building atop an unnamed mountain north of Missoula.

Everything appeared to be going well until the new TV station signed on in July of 1954. The TV sets in and around Missoula received more "ghost" signals than anyone could count, resulting in a distorted picture in the city and surrounding area. However, the village of Darby, 60 miles to the south, received a clear, watchable picture. The problem was compounded when the new Cable TV system in Missoula refused to carry channel 13, electing instead to offer three Spokane channels, along with one each from Butte and Salt Lake City.

The early KGVO-TV engineering and production crews were required to transport themselves, along with film, commercial copy and slides to the mountain top, either by four-wheel drive vehicle or snow cat, depending on the season. This continued until a suitable microwave (STL) link was made practical between the downtown offices and the transmitter site on "TV Mountain." The crews sometimes lived atop the peak for a week at a time, under very primitive and sometimes unsanitary conditions.

As the station's problems grew, Mosby sold his KGVO Radio to the Western Broadcasting Company, and the television station became KMSO-TV. The problems with the Cable TV company were eventually resolved and they carried a "ghost free" channel 13 picture on the system. Viewers in the outlying areas were still plagued with ghosting if they had to watch a direct signal.

Even when the litigants for channel eight all dropped out of the contest, Mosby went against the advice of his engineers and refused to apply for the lower channel, where the ghost problems would not be so intense. The Montana Television Network eventually built KPAX (TV) on channel eight in Missoula.

In the early 1960s, RCA pioneered their "traveling-wave" antenna for TV and KMSO was selected as the first station to install the new revolutionary radiating device that promised to reduce ghosting. In the spring of 1962 installation of the new antenna began at the KMSO transmitter site atop "TV Mountain." All went well until the crew placing the new antenna on the KMSO tower let a line snap and the new radiator plunged to the ground, breaking into pieces.

KMSO Program Director Hugh "Huge" Bader later admitted there was only one thing worse than the accident. That was having to go into A.J.'s office and tell him about it. Bader was also Mosby's son-in-law.

Almost exactly a year later, another attempt was made to install a second T-W antenna at the mountain top site. An identical accident took place and the replacement antenna was dropped several hundred feet and destroyed. Bader went across the street for a couple of stiff drinks before he got the courage to face Mosby the second time.

Today, Channel 13 is KECI (TV) and operates with state-of-the-art antennas and places a good signal into Western Montana. Mosby went to his reward and Bader went to Channel eight in Billings.

In the early 1960s, KOOK-TV (now KTVQ) in Billings began swapping local programming with KRTV (Great Falls) and KXLF-TV (Butte) through a micro-wave link between the stations. This interconnection eventually became the Montana Television Network (MTN). KPAX at Missoula was added in June of 1970.[104] The Missoula station operated as a fulltime satellite of KXLF until 1976.

The Eagle Communications Network (Western Montana News) had its beginning when KECI (TV) (formerly KGVO-TV) built KTVM at Butte. KTVM signed on May 12, 1970 as a full-time satellite of KECI (TV). KCFW at Kalispell, which had been on the air for some time, was added to the network later. KTVM became a semi-satellite in 1982 and now originates most of its non-network programming.

Montana's first UHF TV station, KTGF (TV) began operation on channel 17 in Great Falls during the summer of 1986. The new station was plagued with an unusual problem. As soon as their transmitter was turned on, half the garage door openers in Great Falls activated because their operational frequency was very close to channel 17.

Today, several construction permits exist across Montana for UHF stations and many have expired due to lack of interest and financing.

Late in 1991, KTVQ at Billings followed the lead of many major market TV stations by becoming a 24 hour operation, programming the "All News Channel" network. Cross-town competitor KULR (TV) went to a 24 hour schedule the next day, followed by many other Montana stations. KTVQ's switch to 24 hours was accompanied by much on the air promotion, proclaiming their debut as "Montana's First 24 Hour TV Station."

11

Broadcasters' Problems

Two of the greatest problems facing Montana broadcasters are the immense distances within the Treasure State and the relatively small population. The first-time visitor to the Big Sky Country is appalled by the incredible mileages between towns and cities. Even in Great Falls, the state's second largest metro area, a person can drive from a very crowded neighborhood into a wheat field in a matter of a few blocks, with no prospect of another city of any size until Lewistown, 110 miles away.

One of Montana's television pioneers, P.N. Fortin, stood atop the Rimrocks on the eastern edge of Billings, alongside the KGHL-TV transmitter building and made the comment, "Look at all those rabbit ears!" He was not facing toward the receiving sets in the city, but looking into the uninhabited plains and hill country to the south and east. It has been said, "In Montana you have to broadcast to a lot of gophers and rabbits in order to reach a few people."[105]

Except for stations in the five or six major cities in Montana, it is generally unprofitable for the local broadcasters to rely on income exclusively from their city of license. They must reach out into the outlying communities for revenue sources. This is especially true in smaller markets such as Red Lodge, Baker, Shelby, Forsyth and Deer Lodge. Even at Bozeman, considered a major Montana radio market, several radio stations place a salesman in outlying towns.

Likewise, stations licensed to the suburban or "bedroom communities" such as Belgrade, Whitefish, Laurel and Polson need to look for income from the neighboring larger cities, "just up the road."

Broadcast revenue goes hand-in-hand with the immense distances and low population. While the average businessman and potential advertiser has become aware of the broadcast media as a suitable method of promoting their wares, the Treasure State has never been a place where the businessmen flock to the station's doors to buy time on the air.

Hard economic times in Montana have always signalled a downturn in broadcast income. Ed Craney of KGIR described the situation at Butte during the depression of the 1930s:

"..advertising dropped to nothing and if it wasn't for the national business, we would have closed. I lived in a suitcase, visiting New York, Chicago, Los Angeles, San Francisco."[106]

Even in modern times, radio and TV stations have reported a drop in spot business when bad economic news was reported, when a factory closed or a local industry shut down. One station manager commented, "We have an obligation to report the news, while that same news may cost us business if the local merchants panic."[107]

An increase in the number of broadcast outlets in a particular area, especially radio stations, can cause a decrease in revenue for the existing stations, at least for a period of time, unless the new stations seek untapped sources of revenue.

Rate cutting can also be a great enemy to the time sales market. In 1961, an AM station in Missoula was broadcasting a consistent 35 minutes of commercial time per hour, yet the station closed and went into bankruptcy. Their rate card had dropped so low, about 25 cents per announcement, it became impossible for the station to meet expenses, even if they had broadcast nothing but commercials.[108]

The Montana broadcaster's problems of distance, low population and the lack of income conspire to create another problem; the lack of talent or broadcast professionals. Many talented Montana sales people, announcers, program directors, managers and engineers have left the state to seek employment elsewhere.[109] Until recent years, Montana stations could, or thought they could, afford only to hire beginners in the business. Many broadcast school graduates have held their first jobs in the Treasure State, moving on to greener opportunities in other states once they acquire expertise in the field. Today, the trend has been reversed, at least to a degree. However, a large number of stations still rely on beginners to staff supposedly professional operations.

Broadcast power is another factor limiting Montana radio and TV stations. Montana broadcast pioneers were among the first to fight the AM clear channels, perhaps never realizing the day would come when they themselves would desire higher powered broadcast facilities.

While the AM stations on the Montana prairies carry incredible distances with a power of only a few hundred watts,[110] the hills and mountains in the western part of the state can soak up AM radio signals like a great electronic sponge. In one area, near Ovando, it is nearly impossible to receive two 5,000 watt stations from Missoula, about 35 miles away, while at a different location, a mile down the road, both stations can be heard loud and clear.[111] Anyone driving through the mountains has had this experience while attempting to listen to a car radio. FM stations do not fare much better, with the signals made almost unintelligible in some areas by "multipath" reception problems.[112]

In recent years, the poliferation of new stations has increased the problems associated with competition. Billings, for example, now has 12 radio stations, not counting two in nearby Laurel, along with three TV outlets. Great Falls suffers from a similar problem, boasting ten operating radio stations, along with three TVs.

Bozeman, a two station market before the middle 1970s, now has six radio stations that operate on a commercial basis, two "non-Commercial" FMs, seeking advertising support through "grants," plus one regular TV station and two LPTVs. Missoula is in similar circumstances with nine radio outlets (including one so-called educational station) and three TV broadcast facilities.

Helena and Kalispell boast eight and six stations respectfully along with one TV and several suburban stations offering competition. A second TV in Helena is reported either failing or off the air.

12

Some Never Made It

Throughout the years, construction permits were issued to many prospective broadcasters, but several proposed Montana stations were never built. As mentioned, KMFR at Great Falls merged with KMON before either station went on the air. Art Mosby's KGFT at Great Falls, which also held the call sign KGFM, along with KYES at Butte, were both stillborn before the first spade-full of dirt was turned over. KBFM at Bozeman was well underway when the owner lost interest.

Late in the 1950s, a group of broadcasters secured a construction permit for a station at Kalispell. The project never materialized and the call sign (KYNG) was deleted and later assigned to a station at Coos Bay, Oregon. The Kalispell frequency was subsequently given to KOFI. Also at Kalispell, Suhr Transport Company was granted an FM permit and the call letters KSSR, but it never got on the air. Likewise, KGEZ-TV was only a broadcaster's dream that never came true.

The owner of a ladies apparel store in downtown Missoula was almost the builder of that city's third radio station in the early 1950s. An AM construction permit was issued for a 250 watt station on 1400 kHz, using the call KMSU. The proposed station had no connection with Montana State University (later known as the University of Montana), and the owner of the permit insisted it stood for K-MiSsoUla. The store had a sign in its window promoting KMSU for several years, but it never came to pass, and KBTK became Missoula's third station in 1955.

Other permits were issued to aspiring radio broadcasters at Helena (KCRI-FM), Anaconda, Glendive (KDNC), Red Lodge, and Lewistown. A permit issued to Lewis & Clark Broadcasters at Helena (580kHz-AM) was never built. These permits were in addition to the stations already on the air in the communities, except for the unbuilt Red Lodge permit that antedated KRBN.

When the long "freeze" on TV applications was lifted in 1952, the Rudman-Hyatin Corporation, a North Dakota Company, was issued a permit for channel eight at Billings. They were assigned the call letters KRHT (TV). Construction was delayed until the permit expired. The channel was later assigned to KGHL-TV which today is KULR (TV). Likewise, a permit for channel three in Great Falls for KMON-TV expired.

On June 11, 1984, the FCC granted a construction permit to Big Sky Broadcasters for a 10,000 watt daytime station at Ennis with the call sign KMMD. The station was not built and the permit expired. The 1985 Broadcasting Yearbook indicated Ennis had also been granted a FM permit, licensed to the Madison Valley TV Association with call letters KPCB. No FM channel had been allocated to Ennis at that time and the Madison TV people knew nothing about the station. KPCB remains a mystery, perhaps known only to a computer at the FCC offices.

After the KMMD permit lapsed, Howard and June McDonald of Ennis and Bozeman, doing business as BIG M Broadcast Associates, petitioned the FCC for permission to construct an AM station on 710 kHz. The construction permit was granted October 9, 1986, with call letters KKMT. BIG M also requested that FM channel 254 (98.7 mHz) be allocated to the Ennis area. BIG M applied for the new frequency and this permit was authorized on September 28, 1989. The unwillingness of local landowners to sell or lease property for a transmitter site, coupled with environmental restrictions, last minute financial difficulties and oppressive FCC filing fees, prevented construction of both stations after a seven year effort.

Several permits for TV stations, especially UHFs, have lapsed because the promoters have been unable to secure financing or network affiliation. Among these casualties was the proposed channel 17 in Missoula. The permit was held by James Bender, a Montana broadcast engineer. Bender planned to offer the Missoula area family-oriented TV programming with an emphasis of Christian values. He held the call sign KMSO (TV) which was later assigned to a Missoula FM station.

In 1986, a broadcast group from Sequim, Washington, headed by Luin "Dex" Dexter, received a construction permit to operate KSJM (1520 kHz) at Hamilton. Dexter was unable to construct the station and let the permit expire. He was one of the founders of KLYQ (AM) at Hamilton and later sold the station to local interests.

In 1987, Big Sky Communications of Beaverton, Oregon, applied for 1000 kHz, daytime at Black Eagle, a Great Falls suburb. The applicant asked for the dismissal of the application before a permit could be granted, citing financial problems.

Big Sky was headed up by Verner Nistler, who had dreams of a statewide network, flag-shipped from KBLG at Billings. Nistler also held the permits for KBHG (later KHKR) at East Helena and KZKY (FM) which became KHKR-FM. He also proposed moving KBLG to 890 kHz, from 910, and operating with 50,000 watts. A conflict with a new station in Prince Albert, Saskatchewan blocked the proposal. Nistler's plans for the "Big Sky Network" faded into obscurity.

There have been many instances where applications were submitted to the Federal Communications Commission from parties in Montana which were rejected, usually because of a technical problem. Had Nistler sought 10,000 watts on 890 kHz, his application probably would have been granted.

In 1983 and '84 a group under the sponsorship of the Florence Bible Church received construction permits for several low-power FM stations that would have been located in the state's larger cities. The group operated under the mantle of the Montana Educational Foundation and later transferred the permits to the University Educational Foundation, a paraorganization. A series of delays plagued the Foundation and all the permits expired. A request for reinstatement was opposed by the Yellowstone Public Radio group of Billings (KEMC supporters) early in 1987 and the FCC denied the request for extensions.

The proposed stations would have been: KMMB (89.5 mHz), Helena; KMTT (90.5 mHz), Butte; KMEA (91.1 mHz), Bozeman and KCMF (91.9 mHz), Great Falls. Applications were submitted, but never granted, for new stations at Missoula, Billings and Kalispell. They would have carried satellite-fed programming from the American Heritage Satellite Network of San Diego (now defunct).

In March of 1991, the FCC cancelled permits for educational KBFT (FM) at Browning (88.7 mHz) and KFLN-FM (100.5 mHz) at Baker because of inaction by the permittees. Likewise, the CP for KDRF (FM) of Deer Lodge was cancelled a year later. The station had been on and off the air, operating under a construction permit, but never licensed. The permit for a new FM at West Yellowstone (KRGS at 96.5 mHz) was also cancelled because of inaction. Since then, KWYS has applied for the channel.

May of 1993 saw the deletion of the permit for KYYC (97.9), Shelby. Several other Montana CPs will probably never be built, including three proposed stations at Great Falls: KMCW (1490 kHz), KFTC (FM) at 107.3 mHz and KOOZ (FM 100.3 mHz). The fates of several other Montana CPs are questionable.

13

Montana Call Letter Miscellany

People who are not associated with the broadcast industry are often amazed at those who are and their ability to recall an infinite number of call letters associated with various radio and TV stations. In addition to being a part of the jargon or trade language of the business, a call sign is, for all-purposes, a station's name, as well as its legal identification. And, while some stations have chosen to ignore their call signs, except where required to use them, and identify with pseudonyms such as: "Y-93," "B-98," "The Fox" or "The Cat," most stations still cling to those letters, assigned by the F-C-C, as their trade marks. Most Montana call letters have at least some significance.

The state's oldest radio outlet, KEIN, was originally KFBB. When Frank A. Buttrey established the station on the top floor of his Havre store in 1922, he petitioned the Department of Commerce (which was in charge of radio at the time) for the call sign KFAB, signifying his initials. However, those letters were already assigned to a station in Lincoln, Nebraska. Several contemporaries of Buttrey have passed on the story that Herbert Hoover, then Secretary of Commerce, had opportunity to review the application. Hoover suggested the call sign KFBB as an alternative, an acronym suggesting, "Keeping Frank Buttrey Broke." Buttrey moved the station to Great Falls in 1929 and prospered in spite of Hoover's prediction.

The story may be apocryphal, because the Department of Commerce was assigning call letters from the "KF" area of the alphabet at that time to stations such as KFDC, Spokane and KFKX in Nebraska that began in 1922.

In radio's early days, unless a station requested some particular call sign, the regulatory agency assigned them from an alphabetical list of availabilities. An interesting historical sidelight is the fact that when the first nine radio stations in Montana are arranged in their chronological order, they are also in alphabetical order, even though some of the call signs were requested: KDYS (Great Falls), KFBB (Havre), KGCX (Wolf Point), KGEZ (Kalispell), KGHL (Billings), KGIR (Butte), KGVO (Missoula), KPFA (Helena) and KRBM (Bozeman).

Other Montana call signs are not without significance. In 1954, station KRJF at Miles City, in the heart of the state's cattle country, became KATL, "The Cattle Call."

The third modern-day radio station at Butte was KOPR, "Copper." It seems the KOPR call letters have been used by four different stations in Montana. In 1953, the Butte radio outlet built a TV station and christened it KOPR-TV. The television endeavor lasted just a little more than a year before it succumbed to harsh competition. Later, in 1964, when the radio station merged with cross-town competitor KBOW, the resulting station chose the KBOW call sign. The designation was then acquired by KARR-FM at Great Falls and used until 1978 when the station was sold and became KOOZ. At that time, KBOW reclaimed the call letters for its FM outlet, and KOPR returned to Butte.

KSEN at Shelby, close to the Blackfeet Indian reservation, was at first KIYI, a sound supposedly made by "Indians of the warpath." KTNY (FM) at Libby is "Kootenai," in honor of the river and national forest.

Several Montana stations have attempted to identify with their county of license, with combinations such as KFLN (Fallon County) at Baker; KRBN (Carbon) at Red Lodge; KPRK (Park) in Livingston; KGLT (Gallatin) at Bozeman; KBOW (Silver Bow), Butte and KDZN (Dawson), Glendive.

Montana towns have been immortalized by call signs such as KANA (Anaconda), KHDN (Hardin), KDRG (Deer Lodge), KALS (Kalispell), KGLE and KIVE (Glendive), KBOZ plus KBZN and KBMN (Bozeman), KDLN (Dillon), KCAP (The Capital City), KMSO (Missoula), KCTB (Cut Bank), KSDY (Sidney), KWYS (West Yellowstone), KBLG (Billings) and KAVR (Havre). One set of call letters that was a "natural" for its proposed city of license was KGFM (Great Falls, Montana), but the station was not built and the call sign was given to a station at Bakersfield, California.

It is not difficult to envision KGVW at Belgrade as indicating "gross vehicular weight," but the first owners, King's Garden of Seattle, reported the call is an acronym for "King's Garden Valley Workers."

Montana's several educational stations look to their parent schools for call sign inspiration. These include KEMC (Eastern Montana College), Billings; KMSM (Montana School of Mines), Butte;[113] KRER (Career Institute), Billings; KHTC (Helena Vocational and Technical Center); KUFM (University of Montana), Missoula; KNMC (Northern Montana College), Havre; and KUSM-TV (Montana State University), Bozeman as well as KECC (Custer Community College), Miles City.

Two pioneer Montana stations, both of which have changed their call letters since their inception in the late 1930s, had original combinations that addressed their ownership. KBLL at Helena was KPFA, which signified their parent corporation, "The People's Forum of the Air." In a similar manner, KMMS at Bozeman began as KRBM, offering tribute to Robin B. MacNab, one of the station's stockholders.

KOOK at Billings was not named after someone named Cook. Rather, the station's first manager, K. O. Mac Pherson, was honored by the call sign. The owner selected the letters to indicate that, "K. O. is O-K."

Many Montana stations have taken four-letter combinations that resemble easily remembered words, such as: KQDI (cutie), Great Falls; KBLL (cable), Helena; K'MON, Great Falls; KURL and KULR, Billings; KOFI (coffee), Kalispell; KYLQ and KLYC (click) at Hamilton and Laurel; KOYN (coin), Billings; KSEN (kissin') and its FM companion KZIN (cousin), Shelby; KYSS (kiss), Missoula; KAAR (car), Butte; KATH (cat), Bozeman; KYOT (coyote), Great Falls, which at one time was KARR; KRYK (crick), Chinook; KYUS (cayuse) at Miles City; KOUS (cows), Hardin; KZOQ (zoo), Missoula; KEIN (keen), Great Falls; KLTZ (kilts) and KLAN, Glasgow, KYLT (kilt), Missoula; KIKC (kick), Forsyth; KOOZ and KOHZ (both cozy) at Great Falls and Billings; KLCY (classy), Missoula; KKUL (cool) at Hardin which had been KYTY (Kitty); KFXZ (foxy), Kalispell; and KRKX (Kay-rocks), Billings, KGRZ (kay-griz), Missoula honors the University of Montana athletic teams while KSCY at Belgrade is Kay-sky, a tribute to the "Big Sky Country."

Station KERR, Polson, was named after a nearby landmark, Kerr Dam and KCTZ (TV), Bozeman is supposedly "cats."

The call signs of two Montana stations had a phonetic significance that apparently never occured to those who requested them. Soon after its debut on the air, KTXX became known locally, especially among its Whitefish and Kalispell competitors as "Kotex." The call sign was subsequently changed to KSKR (Kay-skier). In a similar circumstance, KQRR at Ronan switched to KQRK after listeners began referring to it as "Queer."

Helena's KHKR-FM was originally assigned KZKY which was "Kay-sky." KHKR has been represented at "kicker."

Other call letters with various degrees of meaning include: KECI (TV) (Eagle Communications, Inc.), Missoula; KCFW, Kalispell, Columbia Falls and Whitefish; KMCM (Miles City, Montana); KMMR (Malta, Montana Radio); KTGF (Television Great Falls) and KTVM (TV Montana), Butte.

KAAK (K-99) at Great Falls was originally KANR, paying homage to Frank Anderson, the original owner. Montana's pioneer FM, KPWD at Plentywood, honored the town, while KBGF (now KMSL) expressed the slogan, "Keep Building Great Falls." KLCB at Libby honors its ownership, the Lincoln County Broadcasters.

In an attempt to give the impression of a three-letter call sign, KUUS at Billings became "Kay-Double-Ewe-Ess," or K-W-S. On the other hand, a Bozeman AM/FM combination once held the call sign KUUB and preferred to be called "Cube." KKMT at Ennis would have been K-M-T, except for official station IDs.

The state's postal abbreviation (MT) has been enshrined on the call letters of KMTX and KZMT, both at Helena, as well as KMTA, Miles City along with the proposed KKMT.

At Billings, a radio outlet and TV station have been confused for years. Radio is KURL (curl) while the TV is KULR (Color). There is no connection between the stations.

Others with some degree of significance include: KGPR (Great Falls Public Radio) and the proposed KBFT (Blackfeet) at Browning. Call signs such as KOJM and KPQX (Havre), KGHL and KIDX (Billings), KGEZ (Kalispell), KRJF (Miles City), KGCX (Sidney), KGIR (Butte) and KDXT (Missoula) have no known significance.

The old KBMY signified Billings-Montana-Yellowstone, while KDBM indicates Dillon-Beaverhead-Montana.

One station attempted to make something out of its call sign after it was assigned to the station. Art Mosby, the original owner of KGVO at Missoula, sought to link the "GV" in the station's call letters to the five "Great Valleys" that converge at Missoula, but records indicate the letters were assigned by the Federal Radio people from a list of available calls. The tie-in was definitely after the fact.

There have been a few stations in Montana with very similar call letters. One example is KRBM at Bozeman and KRBN, Red Lodge. Fortunately, the signs were not in use at the same time. Both stations operated on 1450 kHz. Bozeman's KRBM changed to KXLQ in 1946, fifteen years before KRBN began. There was a time overlap between KXLL in Missoula and KXXL, Bozeman. KXXL was changed from KXLQ when it was purchased by Richard Smiley's Double-X Broadcasters. Both KXXL and KXLL were linked together in the final days of the Z Bar Net before it folded and the stations were sold by Ed Craney and his associates to various individuals.

Lewistown's KXLO was easy to confuse, on sight, with KXLQ, but the Lewistown station was never a part of the Z Bar Net. In fact, they were assigned KXLO before the Z Bar stations adopted the "XL" prefix.

KBMJ (FM) at Hardin has held more call signs than any other Montana station. It began as KRWS (FM), then became KHDN-FM, KATM, KBSR-FM, KGHL-FM, KDWG, and then KBMJ. For a short time, it was also KKUL-FM.

The call letters KMSO have been all over Missoula. They were first acquired by KGVO-TV when A.J. Mosby sold KGVO radio to Western Broadcasting and needed a new call sign for the TV outlet. Later, when Western purchased KMSO, they changed back to KGVO-TV. In the

1980s, a successful applicant for channel 17 at Missoula, James Bender, selected KMSO as his call. When the permit expired, a local FM station (KUEZ), took KMSO. MSO is the aeronautical designation for Missoula used by the airlines and the F-A-A.

An interesting story centers around the call sign KBSO. In radio's early days, the frequencies immediately above the broadcast band were used by police and fire agencies. These stations were given three and four letter signs just like broadcast and shortwave stations. During this time, the Bozeman Police and Gallatin County Sheriff shared a law enforcement radio license that was assigned the designation KBSO, "Bozeman Sheriff's Office." In the 1950s, police facilities were moved to VHF and UHF frequencies, and given three letter/three number call signs. Bozeman lawmen were assigned KTX799 and KOA404. KBSO was retired.

At Laurel in 1987, new owners revived a station that had been silent for nearly two years, using the KBSO call letters. The facility had previously been KNFL, a station with a sports emphasis, and KLYC prior to that. The new "BSO" designation referred to the "Big Sky Oldies" format of the station. It became KFBN (Business News) and is now KBSR.

Many call letter combinations, once native to Montana, are now in use outside the Treasure State. KGIR was a station at Cape Girardeau, Missouri. KRBM is a non-commercial entity at Pendleton, Oregon, while KPFA is a listener supported FM at Berkeley, California. KXLQ and KXLK are in Indianola, Iowa and Haysville, Kansas. The infamous KTXX was taken by an unsuspecting station in Devine, Texas.

KSTR, a call sign originally given to KXLK (now KXGF) at Great Falls, has been in use for several years at Grand Junction, Colorado, where it is known as "Kay Starr."

Montana's classic call letters, KOOK, have been used by both an AM and FM station as well as a TV outlet. In 1972, Joe Sample of the Montana Television Network (MTN) sold KOOK Radio, which retained the call sign. Channel two needed a new identification, so Sample and his manager, Don Bradley, ran a nation-wide contest asking broadcasters to submit their ideas. The field was narrowed to 15 entries (some of which were already in use) and the staff at KOOK-TV selected KCMR (TV) for Charles M. Russell, the cowboy artist. However, the management soon decided "Charlie" Russell was more identified with Great Falls than Billings, and selected KTVQ (which rhymes with "two") as the new identity, leaving no clear winner. The grand prize was a "custom prefab outhouse," minus holes, which "could not be shipped out of Montana."[114]

In the spring of 1988, Citadel Communications purchased KOOK Radio (which had become an FM station) and its AM companion KBIT. KOOK was retired and the two stations became KCTR AM and FM. KOHZ at Billings obtained permission to use the "Cook" call letters, but never used them, electing to remain "Cozy." In September, 1988, KHYV at Modesto, California became KOOK. Both the new KOOK (KHYV) and KCTR (the old KOOK) operate on 970 kHz. After Billings' KOYN became KBLG in 1986, a station at Paris, Texas was awarded the "Coin" letters.

The proposed FM station at Ennis was originally assigned KKHJ in honor of the majority owners, Howard and June McDonald.

In recent years, KZLS (FM), Billings became KKBR (the Bear); KQDI, Great Falls switched to KMSL (Missile); KCTR, Billings adopted the call KDWG (the Dog), a designation that had been used by crosstown KBMJ (FM). Billings' KUUS became KMAY following is acquisition by May Technical College while a new station in Kalispell took the designation KDBR (De Bear). KZLO (AM), Bozeman (formerly KBMN) is now KOBB (Ol' Bob).

Indeed, where will it end?

Former Call Signs of Montana Stations

Present call sign	Former call sign(s)			City
KAAK (FM)	KANR (FM)			Great Falls
KAAR (FM	KJLF (FM)			Butte
KATH (FM)	KBOZ-FM	KBZN (FM)		Bozeman
KATL	KRJF			Miles City
KATQ	KHPN	KATQ		Plentywood
KATQ-FM	KPWD (FM)			Plentywood
KBBZ (FM)	KFXZ (FM)			Kallispell
KBKO (FM)	KOHZ (FM)	KOOK (FM)+	KOHZ (FM) KKLO (FM)+	Billings
KBLG	KOYN			Billings
KBLL	KTCM	KBLL	KXLJ KPFA	Helena
KBMC (FM)	KPXB (FM)+			Bozeman
KBMG (FM)	KLYQ-FM			Hamilton
KBMJ (FM)	KDWG (FM)	KGHL-FM	KKUL-FM KBSR-FM	
		KATM (FM)	KHDN-FM KRWS (FM)	Hardin
KBOZ	KKLO+			Bozeman
KBOZ-FM	KATH (FM)	KYBS (FM		Livington
KBSR	KFBN	KBSO	KNFL KLYC	Laurel
KCAP	KFDW			Helena
KCFW (TV)	KULR (TV)+			Kalispell
KCTR-FM	KOOK (FM)	KBIT (FM)	KOOK-FM	Billings
KDBM	KDLN	KDBI	KDBM	Dillon
KDBM-FM	KDLN-FM	KDLN (FM)	KDBM-FM	Dillon
KDRF (FM)	KDLI+			Deer Lodge
KDWG	KCTR	KBIT	KOOK	Billings
KDZN (FM)	KGLE-FM	KIVE (FM)		Glendive
KECI (TV)	KGVO-TV	KMSO (TV)	KGVO-TV	Missoula
KEIN	KKGF	KFBB		Great Falls
KGRZ	KGMY	KXLL		Missoula
KHKR	KVCM	KHKR	KBHG+	East Helena
KHKR-FM	KZKY (FM)+			East Helena
KIDX (FM)	KBMS (FM)			Billings
KIKC-FM	KXXE (FM)			Forsyth
KKBR (FM)	KZLS (FM	KKOZ (FM)	KURL-FM	Billings
KKUL	KBSR	KYTY	KHDN	Hardin
KLCB	KOLL	KLCB		Libby
KLCY	KYSS			Missoula

KMAY	KUUS	KBMY			Billings
KMMS	KUUB	KXXL	KXLQ	KRBM	Bozeman
KMMS-FM	KMMS (FM)	KUUB-FM	KUUB (FM)	KHTK (FM)+	Bozeman
KMON	KMFR+				Great Falls
KMON-FM	KNUW (FM)				Great Falls
KMSL	KQDI	KUDI	KBGF		Great Falls
KMSO (FM)	KUEZ (FM)				Missoula
KMTA	KCCA+				Miles City
KMTX-FM	KPEF (FM)+				Helena
KMXE (FM)	KAFM (FM)	KBSV (FM)+			Red Lodge
KNMC (FM)	KNOG (FM)				Havre
KOBB	KZLO	KBMN			Bozeman
KOPR (FM)	KBOW-FM				Butte
KQDI-FM	KOOZ (FM)	KOPR (FM)	KARR-FM		Great Falls
KQRK (FM)	KQRR (FM)				Ronan
KRKX (FM)	KFBA (FM)				Billings
KRSQ (FM)	KTWM (FM)				Laurel
KRTV (TV)	KCTL (TV)+				Great Falls
KSCY (FM)	KGVW-FM	KCDQ (FM)	KMZK (FM)	KGVW-FM	Belgrade
KSEN	KIYI				Shelby
KSKR	KTXX				Whitefish
KSVI (TV)	KPQD (TV)+				Billings
KTNY (FM)	KVAD (FM)				Libby
KTVH (TV)	KTVG (TV)	KTCM-TV	KBLL-TV	KXLJ-TV	Helena
KTVQ (TV)	KCMR (TV)+	KOOK-TV			Billings
KULR (TV)	KGHL-TV				Billings
KVCK	KTYX	KVCK			Wolf Point
KVCK-FM	KTYX-FM	KVCK-FM			Wolf Point
KVCM (FM)	KVYJ (FM)				Helena
KXGF	KYOT	KARR	KXLK	KSTR+	Great Falls
KXTL	KCEZ	KXLF	KGIR		Butte
KYLT	KQTE	KBTK			Missoula
KYYA (FM)	KOYN-FM				Billings
KZLO (FM)	KZLO-FM	KZLO (FM)+			Bozeman
KZMT (FM)	KCAP-FM				Helena
KZOQ (FM)	KYLT-FM				Missoula

+ - Assigned by the FCC but never used on air,

NOTE: At least 70 Montana stations have changed call signs since first coming on the air or prior to their air date. Some abandoned call letters have been picked up by other stations.

14

Slogans

Many Montana stations, especially the pioneer outlets, placed a great emphasis on slogans, both as an alternate method of identification and as a form of self-promotion. KFBB relied heavily on its longevity with such phrases as, "Serving Northern Montana since 1922," and "Montana's Oldest Radio Station." KGIR at Butte became known as the "Voice of Montana," even though the station covered only a portion of the state's western area. Bozeman's KRBM was "The Yellowstone Park Station," a slogan that was also a misnomer, inasmuch as they did not get a good signal into the park.

KGVO was "The Voice of the Five Great Valleys," while in Billings, KGHL promoted its ownership as "The Northwestern Auto Supply Company Station." KATL at Miles City was the "Cattle Call."

KPFA (later KXLJ) claimed the title, "The Capital City Station," until they were no longer the only radio voice in Helena. KMON was the "Montana Farmer-Stockman Station." KXLL took great pride in being "Radio Montana," in spite of the fact they barely put a signal into all of Missoula county with their 250 watts. At Great Falls, KXLK was the "Voice of the Electric City."

Billings listeners heard, "This is Kook...Kay...Double Oh...Kay," and KXXL in Bozeman identified as "Kay.Double Ex..El!" Both stations were eventually ordered to stop using this method of identification. The FCC asserted it sounded like KWOK and KWXL.

At Red Lodge, KRBN was, "The Big Country Sound in the Big Sky Country," a slogan that was picked up by KBOW at Butte. Others included: "The CBS Station at the Top of the Nation (KFBB)," "Five-thousand watts That Sound Like a Million (KGVO)," "U-R Listening to K U-R L, Billings," and who can forget the mellow voice of Ed Cooney making a station break, "This is Copper, K O P R, Butte."

KFBB was not alone in promoting its network affiliation as a part of their station identification. For years, KGHL identified as, "NBC for the Midland Empire." KGVO was, "CBS for Western Montana," while other stations used similar "promos" with their call letters.

The Z Bar Net used a unique slogan for a while in the 1950s. At the end of each Z Bar originated program, the network cue was given as, "This is the Montana Broadcasters....Z Bar Net...The Treasure State Network." Listeners were left wondering which of the three it really was! In previous years, it had been, "This is Montana's Radio Network, The Z Bar Net," followed by the NBC chimes played on a small xylophone.

KGVO had a series of one-liners they used in conjunction with their station identification, such as "At the Heart of the Five Great Valleys." One Thanksgiving Day, when the staff members had taken turns on and off the air, so everyone could be with their families for the holiday dinner, staff announcer Pat Connell came on the air with, "Where the announcers are Stuffed With Turkey.......This is KGVO, Missoula!"

While it was not an "on-the-air" promotion, KXXL at Bozeman made heads turn in the late 1950s with a billboard promotion they initiated along the roads coming into the city. The signs proclaimed for all to see, "Mister Traveler, While You Were Away, We Spent Many Pleasant Hours With Your Wife!.....KXXL."

In the early 1960s, KOOK Radio at Billings went to a "Top-40" or Rock and Roll format and hired a batch of young DJs who called themselves the "Kooky KOOK Good Guys!" KRBN immediately replied with, "This is KRBN, Red Lodge, Where Everyone is a 'Good Guy' not just the Radio Announcers."

Of course, there were always the fulltime stations in Montana that made a bit of fun at the daytime-only stations by salting their station breaks with, "We don't run down at Sundown!"

Montana stations were known to take an occasional swipe at the local newspapers with such slogans as:

"Remember.....when you hear it, its NEWS, when you read it, its HISTORY."

Or, how about this thought provoking statement,

"We have to give it to the newspaper, you can't wrap your garbage in your radio." (Or, line the bottom of your bird cage....etc.!)

One station that wasn't afraid to jab their competition on the air made this statement:

"That other station in town is completely automated. Absolutely nothing can go WRONG......wrong.....wrong......wrong......wrong!!!!!"

In August of 1986, soon after their debut on the Bozeman airwaves, KUUB (FM) began using the slogan, "Music of Your Life." They were almost immediately contacted by Al Hamm, syndicator of the format of that name, who spoke seriously of a law suit. KUUB soon came up with something similar, but different!

15

Christian Radio

During the first decades following the establishment of pioneer radio stations in Montana, the Sunday morning church service broadcast was as much a part of the station schedules as the six o'clock news or the morning farm report. Many stations also welcomed the syndicated Gospel programs to their Sunday schedules, not only for inspirational purposes, but also as a steady and reliable source of revenue because the Christian organizations paid for their time on the air, just like the secular advertiser.

Several of the state's leading stations such as KFBB, KGHL and KGCX carried the "Back to the Bible Broadcast," from Omaha, Nebraska six days a week in prime morning time for many years.

As years passed, some station managers began to look upon both the church broadcasts and the syndicated offerings as simply "audience losers" and "sources of controversy." In addition, many managers and program directors felt the Sunday morning time could be better spent offering popular music and their regular commercial advertising because it "had a greater appeal."[115]

These negative feelings toward the "Gospellers" or "Holy Joes" as they were called, finally surfaced during the late 1950s in the Bozeman area when a church at Belgrade was denied access to a local station.

Pastor Harold Erickson of the Christian and Missionary Alliance Church at Belgrade spearheaded an effort to establish a Christian radio station in the area that "would provide wholesome music and inspirational programs." The result of this undertaking was KGVW, which took to the air February 2, 1959 under the aspices of King's Garden, Inc. of Seattle, a Christian group that was already operating a station in that area. In 1962, KGVW's license was transferred to Christian Enterprises, Inc. (CEI), a Montana Corporation, headed by Erickson and several businessmen in Montana, including Rev. Alvin House of Bozeman.[116]

The station received an immediate warm welcome from the evangelical Christian community in Southwestern Montana, but was not without its detractors. Mainly because of its emphasis on Gospel or "religious" programming, KGVW unjustly earned the reputation as the "Dutchman Station," a reference to the fact that many people of Dutch descent in the nearby communities of Amsterdam and Churchhill were "very religious," therefore a religious station must be connected with them.[117]

Actually, most of the theology and religious teaching heard on KGVW's programs, such as "The Back to the Bible Broadcast" and "The Radio Bible Class," was at odds with the extreme Calvinism and Amillennialism taught by the Dutch Reformed Church, although many of the Dutch businessmen advertised on the station.

In January, 1962, CEI purchased KURL at Billings, a 500 watt daytime station that had been through a series of owners and a variety of formats and was ready to go silent. Erickson and his helpers moved the studios for KURL from a downtown location to the transmitter site in southeast Billings. A few months later, the downtown building burned to the ground. CEI's corporate headquarters was eventually set up in Billings alongside KURL.

A request from a Christian businessman's group in Glendive for Erickson to establish a station there, resulted in KGLE which began on August 22, 1962.

A supposed demand for Gospel programming resulted in the purchase of KXLL at Missoula by CEI in 1963. The station had been off the air for about a year. Erickson and his associates remodeled the station, updated some equipment and went on the air as KGMY. Following a series of problems, coupled with difficulty in obtaining advertising and other support, the station was sold to another Christian-oriented group apart from CEI. This new company also experienced a lack of support from the evangelical community of Missoula and KGMY was eventually sold to a secular broadcaster. The station exists today as KGRZ.

CEI constructed KALS (FM) at Kalispell in 1974 and it became CEI's only fulltime Gospel FM. KALS has prospered, but the purchase of KARR at Great Falls did not excite the Christian churches and business men of the area. KARR was eliminated from the CEI quiver in 1982 and sold to secular operators. It became KYOT and then KXGF.

The CEI group has owned and operated stations in North Dakota, New Mexico and Wyoming, but their main thrust has been in Montana.[118]

Along with the Gospel stations, Christian Enterprizes also built KGVW-FM at Belgrade (now KSCY), KURL-FM (now KKBR) and KIVE(FM) at Glendive which became KDZN. These stations were programmed with a beautiful music format with very little inspirational material. The three FMs have been sold by CEI, mainly to obtain revenue for their other radio endeavors. The Belgrade FM was reclaimed in 1987 after a default and resold in 1994 to cross-county competitor KMMS.

A separate entity, Hi-Line Radio Fellowship, Inc., offers Christian programming on KXEI at Havre and KVCM, Helena. Before obtaining an

FM permit for 103.1 mHz, Hi-Line leased KHKR (AM) and operated it as KVCM.

In 1958, a group of pastors and Christian businessmen in the area around Great Falls applied to the FCC for a permit to build a Gospel-oriented station at Great Falls. The proposed station would have operated on 730 kHz, daytime, with a directional antenna to protect KURL at Billings. One of the stockholders was a Canadian and the FCC returned the application under its non-alien clause. The difficulty was never resolved and no permit was issued. Reverend Guy Fry, a pastor from the Conrad area, was a driving force behind the application. Fry had a Sunday morning program called "Gospel Cheer," on KFBB for many years.

A pastor from Stevensville headed-up an organization that planned to construct a group of Christian stations in the early 1980s. Much information on this is found in the section of this treatise entitled: "Some Never Made It!"[119]

In the late 1980s and early 90s, several new Gospel stations began in Montana. October 1988 saw the advent of KJLF (King Jesus Lives Forever) at Butte under the auspices of Maranatha Broadcasters. In 1993 the station sold to Sunbrook Communications (KXTL/KQUY). The Christian programming was discontinued and the station operates today as KAAR (FM). KXEI and KVCM also began in this time period. Several secular Montana broadcasters still carry some Gospel programs and music on Sunday.

In the Spring of 1994, Word-in-Music broadcasters of South Dakota began Christian Contemporary station KRSQ at Laurel-Billings.

Moody Bible Institute has several FM translators in Montana that re-broadcast KMBI-FM at Spokane along with a few satellators (satellite-fed translators) that relay Moody Broadcasting Network from Chicago. Other satellators re-program Family Radio out of San Francisco, and American Family Association Network of Tupelo, Mississippi and KCSP (FM) at Casper WY.

16

Radio & TV News

At the beginning of Montana's broadcast era, most stations offered news, mainly in the form of copy either read directly (or rewritten) from the local newspaper. This was a practice frowned upon by the papers, but the stations asserted, "Once it is printed, it is public information."

There are no records of lawsuits or other legal actions being taken by the publishers against the stations, even though there were clear copyright violations.

Three major news services, United Press, Associated Press and the International News Service, began offering news to radio stations in the 1920s, but this ceased in 1933 because of pressure brought by the papers. Some stations were able to acquire news from Transradio Press, a short wave news service that broadcast from Mexico, transmitting the copy in Morse code. Few Montana stations subscribed to the service, although oldtimers like KGHL's Fritz Bartlett often told stories about long hours copying the news in code.[120]

With the advent of the major networks, stations were able to broadcast coverage of world, national and sometimes regional events through the network newscasts.

In 1940 the problems between publishers and broadcasters were overcome. Montana stations were slow to subscribe until the beginning of World War II, when many stations took on newswires to supplement coverage obtained from the networks. Both AP and UP (later UPI) established Montana news bureaus at Helena and Billings.

As competition increased and new stations began broadcasting, several stations either hired news directors or assigned the local news responsibility to a staff member. A few stations placed a major emphasis on local news reporting and some gained a reputation for news coverage. KGVO became a leader in the field with pioneer newsmen John Rolfson and Don Weston.

Throughout the 1940s and '50s, the Z Bar Net relied on their newsrooms at Butte and Helena, while the other Z Bar stations were served by the several newscasts delivered to the network by KGIR (KXLF) or KPFA (KXLJ).

By the 1960s and early '70s, leading stations in the competitive markets hired newsmen and offered maximum local news reporting. Major markets such as Billings and Great Falls developed excellent news departments that compared favorably to KGVO News.

Newsmen such as Warren Kemper of KGHL and Cato Butler of KCAP lead the way in their cities, following what came to be known as the "Weston Pattern." In the mid 1950s, KFBB lead the local news scene in Great Falls through the reporting of Ron Richards, a Weston disciple.

News departments and reporters were, and still are, difficult to justify simply from a profit and loss standpoint. In recent years, radio stations formerly known for their news coverage have slipped into a state of complacency and relied mainly upon the wire services and newspapers.

Meanwhile, TV stations such as KXLF-TV and KTVQ offered outstanding coverage through news departments headed by Jay Kohn and Gus Koernig. At Bozeman, KBMN excelled in local news for several years in spite of major political/philosophical differences between the news director and station owner. KBMN's news distinctive was eclipsed in 1975 with the advent of a dynamic news operation at newcomer KBOZ. In the Bozeman area, only one or two stations continue to offer excellent news coverage.

News, more than any other programming factor, seems to ebb and flow with the whims of management and the economic situation of the station. In nearly every market, one or two stations continue to dominate the news scene, along with most of the local TV stations that are faced with the intense competition connected with the evening six o'clock news hour.

The single station dominance brought on by newscasters such as Gus Koernig, Don Weston, Jay Kohn and Ron Richards, along with John Russell, Rich Jessen and others in the 1970s and '80s, has not been equalled in recent years. Many radio stations have abducated their news responsibility in favor of the TV competition.

In the late 1980s, the Sunbrook News Network folded because of a lack of interest by both sponsors and stations. Conversely, the Northern Ag-net continues to flourish in both Montana and Wyoming.

17

Montana Broadcasters In Politics

Many Montana broadcasters have been involved in the game of politics at one time or another. Montana broadcast pioneer Edmund "Ed" Craney was perhaps the first to be openly political. Craney made no secret of his admiration and affiliation with Montana's controversial Senator Burton K. Wheeler, who went from a reputation as a "screaming liberal" in his early years in the U-S Senate to what today would likely be considered a "dyed in the wool" conservative in his final years in Congress.

Craney relied on Wheeler's clout to assist him, both openly and behind the scenes in building his radio empire, the Z Bar Network. During the Depression years when NBC threatened to cancel its affiliations in Montana, Craney and Charles Campbell of KGHL enlisted Wheeler's help:

> "Craney made several trips to NBC headquarters. The network wanted $1,500 cash each month. At that time there wasn't $1,500 in Butte, Montana. Finally, Craney turned to Wheeler. The Senator said NBC couldn't be called a national network if they failed to serve every body. The network remained."[121]

Wheeler and Montana's other Senator at the time, Thomas Walsh, used their influence to bring NBC into Montana in the first place around 1930.

Craney and Wheeler remained friends until the Senator's death in 1975. Craney was also close friends with other Montana politicians, many on the state and national level. He and Barclay Craighead were openly associated in ownership of the Z Bar Net, Craighead being a stockholder in at least one of the stations, KPFA (KXLJ) at Helena.

Craighead held several Montana elective offices and was a powerful "behind the scenes" politician until his death. Craney never claimed any political affiliation, and seemed to associate where he pleased and where it was to his advantage.

The Z Bar Net, especially in its early years, was a powerful influence in Montana politics and politicians who incurred Craney's disfavor seldom appeared on his airwaves unless it was in the form of a paid broadcast.

All of Craney's station managers were politically active and one became a candidate for governor of Montana. Pat Goodover originally managed KRBM at Bozeman and was later transferred to the Butte station, KGIR (KXLF). When the Z Bar group built KXLL at Missoula in 1947, Goodover served as the manager for several years until he was assigned to KXLK at Great Falls. Goodover and his associates later purchased KXLK from Craney and set it adrift from the Z Bar as KARR. Goodover obtained a reputation of sorts in Great Falls and was elected to the State Senate for several terms. In 1984, the Republican Party nominated him as its candidate for the governorship to run against extremely popular Ted Schwinden, the Democrat incumbent. Goodover lost to a Schwinden landslide in a year when fellow Republican Ronald Reagan gained a second term without serious difficulty. Goodover retired from politics. It was rumored the G-O-P had selected him as a "sacrificial lamb" in a year when they knew Schwinden could not be defeated by any Republican.

In 1988 another long time member of the State Senate, Stan Stephens, fared much better, defeating two other Republicans in the primary and winning over former Governor Tom Judge, a Democrat. Stephens was the first G-O-P governor in over 20 years in Montana. Judge was a former Helena advertising executive, a field closely related to broadcasting.

Stephens was associated for many years with stations KOJM and KPQX at Havre and a local cable company.

Also in 1988, Montana sent its second Republican to the United States Senate. Conrad Burns, a broadcaster who had been associated with KLYC at Laurel and the Northern Broadcasting System (later the Northern AG Network), scored a resounding and surprise victory over incumbent Democrat John Melcher. Burns had become a well known figure in Montana through his close affiliation with NAG and a multitude of speaking engagements before farm oriented audiences. From his first political stepping stone as a Yellowstone County Commissioner, Burns made the giant leap to the Senate where he is serving with honor but not without controversy. He was re-elected in 1994.

The late Dale G. Moore, president of Western Broadcasting Company, former owner of KGVO, KGVO-TV, KBMN, KCAP and several out-of-state radio and TV stations, had his eye on Montana elective office and was in the process of gaining favor with the conservative wing of the Republican Party before his untimely death in a plane crash. Moore began his climb into right wing ranks in the early 1960s by using his radio stations to broadcast "The National Indignation Convention," a meeting called to protest the training of Yugoslavian pilots in the United States. The ultimate power behind the Convention was the conservative John Birch Society.

Moore served as president of the Montana Broadcasters Association, which has served as a springboard into Montana politics, but he failed to achieve any state or national elective office.

Other Montana broadcasters have attained some degree of political success by being elected to school boards, town and city mayorships and the state legislature. More are undoubtedly waiting in the wings for their political opportunity.

Politics make for strange bedfellows and in Montana some are Broadcasters.

Following his acquisition of KXXL and KWYS, Bozeman broadcaster Richard "Dick" Smiley ran successfully for the Montana state legislature where he served several terms. Smiley was responsible for the bill that changed the name of Montana State University at Missoula to the University of Montana and Montana State College at Bozeman to Montana State University. Republican Smiley's try for the western district congressional seat resulted in defeat and ended his political career.

As a rule, Montana broadcasters venturing into politics have tended to be Republicans, but there are exceptions. Ronald P. "Ron" Richards, a longtime Montana announcer and executive, managed a successful campaign for Democrat Forrest Anderson when he sought the Montana governorship. Richards was rewarded by an appointment as chief of the Montana Highway Department. When Anderson retired, Richards became affiliated with KMTX at Helena until his appointment as chief assistant to Senator John Melcher. He served in that position until Melcher's stunning defeat in 1988.

Montana's favorite son, broadcaster Chet Huntley, retired from NBC in the late 1960s to build and mentor the Big Sky Resort and Ski Area in Gallatin Canyon near Bozeman. Huntley reportedly had a desire to capture either the Montana governorship or a seat in the U-S Senate, but never made his plans public before his untimely death.

Huntley's widow, Tippy, ran in the 1976 primary as a Republican candidate for the U-S House of Representatives, but was defeated. Mrs. Huntley often confided to friends and reporters that Chet was extremely liberal during his days as a network newscaster, but "seemed to become more and more conservative as he grew older." Chet Huntley is the only broadcaster to be enshrined in the Montana Hall of Fame at the Capitol Building in Helena.

18

Oops!!

Throughout the years in Montana broadcasting, the industry has had its share of "bloopers," "fluffs," and downright messups on the air. Perhaps one of the classics happened to a young, unfortunate announcer at Missoula. While he was an outstanding personality, he had the dual bad habits of not prereading his commercial copy and reading everything just as it was written on the page. This lead to some serious embarrassment and the near loss of his job. Early one morning he read a commercial for a local men's clothing store. The copywriter had inadvertently left the letter "r" out of the word "shirt." Sure enough, he read it just as it was on the paper.

The all time radio boo-boo occurred on sleepy Sunday morning at KFBB. At that time, the management of the station insisted that the announcers refrain from wearing headphones, an item that is indispensable if the announcer is to know what he's doing and what is happening on the air. Nevertheless, management prevailed and no headphones were used.

At 10:59 on that Sunday morning, the announcer closed off a syndicated Gospel program, read a commercial and proceeded to introduce the morning service from a Lutheran Church in downtown Great Falls. The actual service usually began a minute or two after eleven and the opening remarks from the studio were read over an interlude of soft organ music. The announcer, Jim Allen, read the introduction, brought up the control that determined the volume of the audio from the church auditorium and proceeded to turn off his mircophone. There was a problem with the mike switch and it did not turn off!

Because the announcer was not wearing headphones, he could not hear the organ music and assumed there was a problem bringing in the church service. With his microphone still on, he pushed back his chair, making a loud squeek, opened the control room door with a loud clank, and, at the top of his lungs called, "Tooooooooonnnnneeee!" to Tony Lopuch, the chief engineer who was working in the shop down the hall. This was all broadcast, including Tony's response from the shop.....

"Whaaaat?" Lopuch quickly determined that the "on-the-air" light was still on, turned off the microphone, and the service continued without further interruption.

For many years after that, when someone needed an engineer at KFBB, they simply called, "Toooooooooonnnnnneeee!"

At KGVO, newsman Robert E. L. Martin had the consistent habit of running into the studio at 12:14:57 pm, just in time to drop into his chair and read the headlines for the 12:15 newscast. Invariably, Martin would pop out of his chair during the first one minute commercial and dash into the newsroom around the corner for something he had forgotten.

These antics were too much for the KGVO announcers. One noon hour, an off duty announcer crept into the studio, right before Martin's newscast, smeared the seat of his chair with rubber cement and managed to flee the scene right before Martin made his usual frantic appearance and came flying into the studio. The newsman plunked himself into the chair and read the headlines. Martin then gave the cue for the commercial, went to dash back into the newsroom to retrive the forgotten item, only to find that he was stuck fast! When the announcer in the control room returned the program to the studio, he and the audience were greeted by a series of unpleasant epithets from Martin, who was attempting to free himself from the chair. The KGVO management went looking for heads, but never found the right ones! (Authors note: "I'm glad they didn't!!!").

During the 1950s, a Great Falls announcer read a section of his news headlines as follows: "The current civil rights bill has been rejected in the Senate, but they plan to introduce a new virgin next week!"

It was January 10, 1947. KPRK at Livingston had just finished an hour-long dedicatory broadcast, marking their first day on the air. A musical program followed. Everything went well until the station's new transmitter shut down. After several minutes of silence, the carrier came back on, and it was obvious to the KPRK audience there was a microphone on somehwere in the building, but no one was aware of it. There were some noises, made by persons moving around the building, followed by a loud voice saying, "Good God, Joe, don't grab that wire, you'll land on your can!" There were a few more moments of silence, and a musical selection came on the air without comment.

Then there was the announcer at Sidney's KGCX who came on the air ruffled and flustered to proclaim, "This is K...G...C...Sid, Exney!"

Kim Potter was one of the best TV announcers who ever worked at KFBB, but he had a tendency to make unintentional spoonerisms. He would transpose the initial sounds of two or more words without knowing it! Potter would occasionally do the weather and predict, "snatter schow snowers." On one occasion, he introduced a fellow announcer as, "Art Weather, the weberman." Perhaps Potter's greatest spoonerism was one he inflicted on himself. One evening he prefaced a newscast with, "Good evening, this is Kim Porter repotting."

Art Weber attracted all sorts of attention, especially that of the sponsor, one night when he was doing a Washington Apple spot on KFBB-TV. Weber concluded the commercial with, ".....always ask for the best of the Washington Apple crap!"

It was fall, and Shelby's KSEN was knee deep in football from the various communities they serve. Jerry Black was doing a game from the town of Choteau. At halftime, during the homecoming ceremonies, a number of people were on hand for the event and were talking on the public address system. Black kept moving over on the bleacher seat to make room for them, and while he was recapping the events of the first half, he fell off the edge of the platform and dropped about 10 feet to the ground, leaving his headphones and mike dangling off the edge. The announcer back at the station heard a distant voice shouting, "We'll be right back after this word."

Also at KSEN, and at another football game, John Lyon had trouble saying Peterson the quarterback. He kept saying, "Peterback the quarterson," much to the dismay of both fans and parents.[122]

At KFBB in Great Falls, the program director had produced an announcement and placed it on the air before a terrible realization came to him. At the place where he intended to say, "For an occasion such as a dinner party, or informal get together," it came out, "Fornication such as a dinner party........"

Pendelton "Pen" Brown was a "Yankee" who moved from the New York/New Jersey area to be Program Director at KFBB-TV. One of his first nights on the air, he read the 11 O'clock news, which contained an item about the various Indian Tribes in Montana. Brown had not pre-read the newscopy and hit the word Assiniboine cold, with no previous knowledge of the Tribal designation.

You'll never guess what he said!

Bob Hauser of KSEN was describing a plane crash and informed his listeners that, "All the survivors died!"

Also at KSEN, Jerry Black invited listeners down to observe a remote broadcast he was doing, where he said they had prepared, "Several urinals of fresh coffee!" Black also has a habit of calling ewes (female sheep) ee-wees![123]

In the mid 1950s, Leo Ellingson was the morning announcer/program director at KFBB in Great Falls. Ellingson was a Montana native and worked the early shift with Farm Director Stan Meyer, an import from the Midwest. One morning, Meyer read a news item that mentioned the nearby town of Ulm and pronounced it Uhlum. Ellingson corrected him, but Meyer insisted he had heard local folks pronounce it that way. Ellingson replied, "Well, the same folks that call it Uhlum also call it Greata Fahls and K-F-uh-B-B!"

Montanans can always tell new announcers from out-of-state: They invariably read news copy from Heleena, Meeger County and the town of Eeenis!

While KGHL announcers were accused of slurring their calls letters to sound like "Cagy as Hell," those at KFBB voiced breaks that came out as, "Cave Be-Be," and guys at KXLF uttered a few "Cakes-El-Eff" station ID's.

While it wasn't an on-the-air goof, an incident occurred at KGVO late in 1962 that deserves note. Earl Morgenroth had just been appointed Station Manager after serving as salesman and Sales Manager. He immediately issued a series of "From the desk of E. Morgenroth" memos that covered everything from office procedure to the proper usage of toilet paper.

Among the epistles was one that declared: "Effective next Monday morning all station employees will wear a white shirt and tie during regular business hours." The memo was directed to the male announcers and salesmen, but nowhere in the memo did it so state.

Vonnie Vaughn, the female office manager, who was no fan of Earl Morgenroth, seized upon the incident. Bright and early Monday morning he walked into the KGVO outer office to find all three female employees at their desks wearing white shirts and ties!

Morgenroth immediately issued an amendment to the "shirt and tie" memo that stated: "This applies to male employees only!" After that, Mister Morgenroth was very careful how he worded his frequent memos.

Also at KGVO, the station program director, was on duty the morning of November 22, 1963 when news came across the network and newswire that President John F. Kennedy had been shot in Dallas, Texas. The Montana Power Company had been running a series of institutional commercials that featured the songs that were popular during World War II and the years that followed. He read the UPI news bulletin concerning the shooting and went back to regular programming which was an MPC commercial that began with the song, "Praise the Lord and Pass the Ammunition."

He had a lot of explaining to do when irate listeners flooded the station phone lines with complaints. He also had a difficult time convincing the manager that the incident was strictly accidental, even though the boss was a Republican.

19

The Author Remembers Radio

Many of my earliest memories center around this thing called radio. It has been a fascination for me since my earliest days. I can still recall the old United Motors (Delco) radio my folks owned. It sat on a table in a very prominent place in the tiny living room of our farm house near Harrison, Montana where I spent my first years. It was powered by a 32 volt DC light plant, something that was rather uncommon in the days when the neighbors had battery powered radios and used "coal oil" and gasoline lanterns to illuminate their homes at night. The battery powered radios were only turned on for a few select programs each day, whereas we could listen any time except when the huge wet batteries were being charged.

At an early age I would climb up on a chair beside the old set and imagine there was a man inside the receiver talking to me, and when an orchestra or choir came on the air, it staggered my imagination to believe they were all inside the set.

When I was very young, my mother explained, as best she could, how radio waves were transmitted great distances from places called "stations" and the people I heard were actually there, not inside the radio. Mom also told me about another miraculous invention just being developed called "television" that would allow us to see the performers and announcer at the station. Such a thing was beyond a young boy's comprehension. Talk coming through the air was one thing, but pictures, never in a million years could such a thing happen.

I can remember the classic NBC chimes coming through the speaker of the old receiving set, and the multitude of wonderful programs that could transport a poor farm boy in Montana to the most wonderful places imaginable.

Perhaps the greatest hero of my boyhood was the "Lone Ranger," and his faithful Indian companion Tonto. At a young age, I learned "Kemo Sabe" meant "faithful friend." It was years before I understood that the music was the "William Tell Overture," and not the "Charge of the Lone Ranger."

And, who can forget the voice of announcer Fred Foy!

"With his faithful Indian companion, Tonto, the daring and resourceful masked rider of the plains led the fight for law and order in the early Western United States. Nowhere in the pages of history can we find a greater champion of justice! Return with us now to those exciting days of yesteryear. From out of the past come the thundering hoof beats of the great horse Silver. A cloud of dust, a firey horse with the speed of light and a hearty cry, 'Hi Yo Silver!' The Lone Ranger rides again!"

I will never forget "I Love a Mystery," heard Monday through Friday evenings on KSL. Jack Packard, Doc Long and Reggie York were real people, not just the product of the mind of the writer, Carlton E. Morse.

When I was a lad, people often told me I resembled Spanky Mac Farland of the "Our Gang" motion picture series. I may have looked like Spanky, but folks said I talked like Froggy, one of the minor characters, a little boy with a deep voice. This enhanced my desire, that when I grew up, "I wanted to be a radio announcer!"

In those days, only the basso profundos were heard on radio. Jackson Beck was my hero. Beck probably had the deepest voice on the air, along with Brace Beamer, who played the Lone Ranger. Beck was the voice behind Bluto, the bad guy in the Popeye cartoons.

The first radio station I ever heard was KGIR. In the daytime we could also hear KGHL at Billings and KFBB, Great Falls. KGIR offered "Lum 'n Abner," a daily feature sponsored by Alka-Seltzer. It was backwoods comedy at its best and a rare day when I missed the adventures of the old boys down at the "Jot 'em Down Store" at Pine Ridge, Arkansas. Later in life I discovered there actually was such a place and paid it a visit!

I was barely nine years old when our family visited the KGIR studios at Nissler Junction west of Butte. What a thrill it was to see the station's transmitter, aglow with the lights of the many large tubes, along with the huge studio where the local programs originated as well as the control room where the announcer sat before the microphone to give the station break: "This is the Voice of Montana.....K G I R.....Butte!"

Arnie Anzjon, owner of a familiar voice and the KGIR general manager gave us the station tour and explained the operation.

Monday night on NBC offered little for a lad my age, because they programmed an evening of classical music, but CBS was a radio paradise! "The Lux Radio Theatre," featuring director Cecil B. DeMille, brought movies to the airwaves, condensed them to one hour and offered free admission to a first run film. An hour later, "The Lady Esther Theatre" did the same thing in half an hour. You could truly say, "I saw it on the radio!"

I remember the other magic programs that came through the airwaves. When I was six years old, my father moved us to Cleveland, Ohio where I was exposed to a city with FOUR radio stations, one for each major network. I can remember the thrill of listening to cowboy "Tom Mix," along with "Captain Midnight," "Jack Armstrong," plus many other great radio dramas on stations WJW, WTAM, WHK and WGAR. Every boy in school had a Captain Midnight secret decoder ring, and I was no exception.

In a second grade classroom I remember hearing a program from an educational station (WBOE) on "FM," a newly developed broadcast service.

When we returned to Montana in 1941, radio played a wonderful part of our lives. As a farm family, now isolated from the big city, except for an occasional visit to Butte or Billings, radio was our window to the world. World War II brought a new meaning to the medium. I remember returning home the afternoon of Sunday, December 7, 1941 to discover the Japanese had made an attack of Pearl Harbor in the Hawaiian Islands. From then on, radio was an essential part of our lives on the little farm near Harrison.

Twice a day, morning and evening, we tuned to KGIR for the very latest newscasts to hear of the developments in the war, and then, at long last, the German and Japanese surrenders in 1945. Throughout the war years, we kept in touch also with the war-centered drama on the radio as the characters we loved so well did their part for the war effort. Bob Hope went to the battle fronts to entertain the troops, and at home other radio stars made the many appeals for us to purchase war bonds and contribute to other efforts that we hoped would end the conflict!

Broadcast history was made the day the NBC Network broadcast "on-the-spot" from the site of the Normandy Invasion of France. At an early age, I determined I would be a part of the great medium called radio.

Comedy was one of the highlights of my radio week, which was often broken up by demands from parents insisting I complete my homework and otherwise prepare for the next day at school. Tuesday nights were anticipated all week because it brought both Bob Hope and Red Skelton to the speaker of our radio from NBC. Later in the week CBS offered a visit with the Bumstead family on "Blondie."

Other radio memories flood my mind as I remember "Fibber Magee and Molly," with a zany cast of characters and the proverbial overstuffed hall closet, a radio soundman's dream, complete with the one last item that fell out and rolled across the floor. "The Aldrich Family," with prodigal son Henry, spoofed the many problems of the teenagers of the day, while each Sunday afternoon brought chilling mystery to the kilocycles with offerings such as "the Shadow," "Gangbusters," and "Nick Carter, Detective."

In late fall, winter and early spring, the hours after school were filled with adventure programs from ABC and Mutual network stations that "skipped" in from the Midwest and Utah. What a variety of adventure it was! Who can forget "Jack Armstrong, the All-American Boy," or the adventures of "Dick Tracy," along with "Superman," starring Clayton "Bud" Collier. Collier's voice always became an octive deeper as he removed his Clark Kent clothing and stated, "This looks like a job for Superman!"

Or, how about "Terry and the Pirates," "The Green Hornet," with his Japanese companion, Kato who suddenly became a Filipino the day after Pearl Harbor? Maybe you remember "Sky King," the cowboy-rancher with an airplane who always rounded up the bad guys before the program was over!

It was truly the era of "The Theatre of the Mind," with the silver-throated baritone and bass announcers on the 50,000 watt clear channel stations proclaiming:

"K-N-X, Columbia Square, Los Angeles, the Voice of Hollywood."
"W-B-B-M Theatre of the Air, Wrigley Building, Chicago.
"The Nation's Station.....WLW, Cincinnati."
"Welcome South, Brother! This is W-S-B...Atlanta!"
"K-O-M-O....The Fisher's Blend Station....Seattle."
"The 50,000 watt Voice of the Middle West...W-H-O, Des Moines."
"This   is   Westinghouse....W-B-Z,   Boston...W-B-Z-A, Springfield."
"The Chicago Tribune Station......W-G-N....Chicago."
and, "W-W-L, New Orleans...Loyola University of the South, with studios in the Roosevelt Hotel."

My parents' move to Missoula in 1946 only whetted my interest in Radio. KGVO, Missoula's only station at the time, had its studios downtown on Front Street, above the Western Montana Press and Radio Club (a private bar). I climbed the stairs to the studios and spent many hours with my nose pressed against the window of the KGVO control room, watching Bud Blanchette, Bill Strothman, Don Hopkins or one of the other staff members making station breaks, reading the news or spinning records from that small booth. The KGVO studios were a show place in those days and a source of wonder to a lad with a sincere fascination with radio. What a pest I must have been to Bud and the others.

Soon after we arrived in Missoula, I met a freckle-faced kid who was a year behind me in school. His name was Ron Richards, and when I found he shared my interest in the airwaves, we became fast friends.

Ron had made acquaintance with a neighborhood radio repairman named Harmon. After much persuasion, we convinced Mister Harmon he should build an illegal radio transmitter for us so we could play radio station (although we didn't say it quite that way).

Harmon built the transmitter, complete with gain controls for two mikes and a couple of turntables. We requisitioned an old table from the nearby flour mill where my Dad worked, and we set up shop in Ron's recreation room (a converted garage), next to his home on Fifth Avenue South.

We were the clandestine voice of the south side and operated two hours after school on weekdays and most of the day on Saturday, playing the few records we owned over and over, and "stealing" network programs from KGVO through a home receiver hooked into our mixer. For a time, the station even owned a primitive wire recorder which we used for "network delay."

We had dreams of constructing a huge, highly directional rhombic antenna that would pick up the network stations in Spokane, but this never materialized. Many fellows, but no girls, came to help. There was Keith Arnold, Jerry Smith and others who all took turns spinning records and being "announcers."

When my family moved to Bozeman, Ron and the boys continued to operate what had become KPOX (illegal call letters for an illegal station), until they decided to change the station's frequency to 640 kilocycles. However, the second harmonic of the KPOX transmitter (roughly 1280 kilocycles) was close enough to KGVO's 1290 frequency that it caused problems in the form of a "heterodyne," or squeal that interfered with KGVO in a good portion of the near southside of Missoula.

Bud Blanchette, KGVO manager, showed up with the sheriff and closed down KPOX. The station returned to the air later, but with much care so as not to interfere with KGVO.

As years passed, interest waned and the KPOX equipment was donated to the Missoula County High School where it served an illegal station known as KONA.

Following High School at Bozeman, I went to work for KXLQ, one of the local stations, where I learned I didn't quite know it all in spite of my clandestine experience as KPOX.

20

Looking Ahead

The decisions made and the trends set within the next few years will irrevocably shape the future of Montana broadcasting. Advancement and development in several areas will help determine that future.

Broadcasting problems associated with the terrain in Montana, especially in the mountainous western section, must be dealt with if the state's radio stations are to have a place in the future scheme of things. A good example of what can be accomplished is the Flathead Valley.

The Flathead has been called "Kilowatt Canyon." Three of the area's five AM stations broadcast with high power. KOFI radiates 50 kW daytime with 10 kW and a directional antenna at night. KERR at Polson has an output of 50,000 watts during the day, while Whitefish's KJJR is using 10,000 watts daytime. Both stations operate with 1,000 watts at night with individual directional arrays.[124] All three stations can be heard throughout the area with very little signal attenuation in the daytime.

Under the Reagan administration, the Federal Communications Commission implemented a program of deregulation that allowed AM stations to utilize frequencies that heretofore had been the FCC's "sacred cows." These channels had been reserved for 50,000 watt outlets in large eastern cities and on the Pacific coast. Several Montana stations are operating on former clear channels, including KOFI at Kalispell; KGVW, Belgrade; KERR, Polson; KJJR at Whitefish and KATL, Miles City.

Many Montana broadcasters remain satisfied with their old regional and local frequencies, along with the 1,000 and 5,000 watt limits imposed on those channels. However, some are beginning to realize higher power could be the answer to some of their coverage problems, especially in the western portion of the state. Greater coverage means a larger potential audience and a greater possibility for advertisers.

Most of the channels opened up in Montana to AM stations require a directional antenna (DA), either at night or on a fulltime basis, depending on the particular frequency and the location of the proposed facility. In the past, DAs have been a problem, both from a technical and operational standpoint. With deregulation, stations are no longer required to have an operator on duty with a first class license during DA hours. Technology has changed to the point where directional arrays are no longer the engineering nightmare they once were.[125]

Several Montana FM stations are locked in on Class "A" channels, and therefore are limited to an effective radiated power (ERP) of 6,000 watts. This means the station is held to a broadcast radius of 30 to 40 miles at the most. This can severely limit a small market FM station. Montana FM operators in the smaller towns need to petition the FCC for class "C" channels in their areas, allowing those stations to operate with up to 100,000 watts ERP. This will mean not only a "harder" signal locally, but also greater potential for listeners in outlying areas.[126]

If a town or area has no local FM service, or if the need for an additional service can be justified, the FCC allows local residents to install low-power translators to rebroadcast the signal from a licensed FM station into an area where it cannot be received otherwise, or where the signal is extremely weak.

Translators have been very effective in extending the service areas of many FM stations in Montana. Some commercial stations have a variety of translators in remote areas. This concept has been used to great advantage by the educational stations in the state, especially KUFM at the University of Montana at Missoula and KEMC at Montana State University-Billings (formerly Eastern Montana College). Student-owned KGLT at Montana State University-Bozeman has also considered a translator cluster.

These translators operate on channels that are not otherwise in use, and are restricted in their power output. They may operate only as long as they do not interfere with established facilities.[127]

FM translators can expand a station's coverage without the expense of higher power or an increase in antenna height.

Many broadcasters have been encouraged by the FCC's authorization of low-power television (LPTV) stations. LPTVs are essentially television translators that are permitted to originate programming and are limited to 100 watts on VHF frequencies and 1,000 watts on UHF.[128] Therefore, LPTV stations in small markets could offer some local programming while relaying a portion of a larger market station's schedule.

A network of LPTVs across the state, much like the old Z Bar network, could be a distinct possibility if the LPTV concept becomes viable.

As this is written, there are many construction permits for LPTV stations in Montana, but few are on the air and operating. Two noteworthy exceptions are KTZ-26 and KBZ-42 at Bozeman which retransmit two Butte stations and provide local programming on a limited basis.

Conventional satellite service is now available to Montana broadcasters. A few years ago, it was beyond comprehension that radio network service could be supplied via satellite, especially intrastate broadcasts. Montana stations are now able to receive satellite service directly from a source within the state.[129]

With that in mind, the potential for Montana news, programming or special events is almost limitless. A Montana station with the proper staff and expertise could furnish programming for smaller, locally owned stations, outside the larger facility's primary coverage area, while also allowing the smaller stations to retain their local image.

Satellite channels could be used for sports and other programs of state-wide interest. A high-powered FM station could carry network programs on its "sidebands" for the benefit of outlying stations.[130] The flagship station could feed news reports and "inserts" much like the service on the present AP and CNN Radio networks. Under certain circumstances FM translators may receive their programming from satellites if the originating station is designated as educational.

Cities and towns in Montana presently considered too small for a local station could hope for radio service in the future. These small market stations could receive both national and state network service, while retaining their local identity. Smaller market stations could be grouped together as a "package" and sold as a combination to potential national and regional advertisers.

Towns such as Roundup, Conrad, Big Timber, Harlowton, Whitehall and several others could potentially have their own radio station.

Even though there are over 60 FM stations in the state, the possibility of new channels being assigned to small communities is almost limitless. The FM band is not crowded in Montana and the space above 100 mHz is wide-open, with only about sixteen stations in the entire state operating in that portion of the spectrum.[131]

Once Montana broadcasters get busy and plan ahead, they may not have to be content with New York or Hollywood-type programming.

Many stations have suffered from a malady called, "The sameness syndrome." T.J. Gilles identified the symptoms of this disorder in a 1983 magazine article:

> "It was during a car trip from Laurel to New York City with a radio on most of the way that I came to an inescapable conclusion: The call letters may change, but the whole USA might as well be one big radio station. Within their genres, the stations play the same songs, and apparently the same jingle companies do all the station logos, changing the call letters and towns, but little else. Things have 'progressed' since that trip a few years ago, with many stations going to an all-bland format with tunes selected and announced by a taped anonymity in Burbank

or LA. One Billings FM station ....includes a voice-modulat-
ing device designed to make all the announcers sound exactly
the same."[132]

Gilles' analysis is at least partially correct. In the past, many stations
in Montana have used the same music services, same jingles and promotional aids and even the same "canned" announcers. The advent of the
national satellite program services has only compounded the problem.
For a time, a Helena FM station and a small AM at Deer Lodge programmed the same music, the same announcers and the same news. Only
the local commercials and station IDs were different. Slowly, stations are
forsaking satellite formats.

Montanans have always been individuals! Why shouldn't their radio
stations be individual? Gilles' article goes on to point out the unmistakable
format of KSEN at Shelby. Should every Montana station strive to be
another KSEN? God forbid! One is enough, but why cannot each Montana
station be itself, not a copy of some station in a far removed major market?

Montana cities and towns are individuals, why not their radio and TV
stations? Butte and Lewistown are as different as two cities can be. Likewise, Red Lodge and Missoula.

Can 14 radio stations in Billings all be different? Certainly! If people
can be different and newspapers can be different, why not 13 or 14 radio
stations? A station at Red Lodge should program differently than one at
Hardin! Red Lodge is a mountain town in a tourist and skiing area. Hardin
is a plains city, surrounded by the Crow Indian Reservation. They had
better be different! Broadcasting formats should be in tune with each
individual area and each particular need of the community they serve.

Professionalism arrived late in Montana. The situation is similar to the
state's law enforcement, which has rapidly evolved from an assortment
of "gun-totin' cowboys" and "Keystone Kops," to some of the most professional deputies and police officers in the nation. An increasing number
of broadcast station managers and owners have at long last seen the
advantage of hiring and paying professional people. Montana has its own
broadcasting school, and while its graduates are by no means professional
radio and TV people the minute they step out the door with a diploma
in hand, it is a beginning toward a professionalism that has been lacking
in Montana.

Unfortunately, station management was many times the chief enemy
and adversary of professionalism in Montana. Many stations hired their
announcers and disc jockeys right off the streets or out of the high schools.
Sometimes, these fledglings performed quite well, and several who began
in this manner are presently in major market situations. This was, many
times, in spite of management, who seemingly resented anyone who
showed more talent than themselves.

Although there were other situations, KFBB was a prime example of an operation that seemingly existed in spite of the shortcomings of the management, especially in the 1950s and early 60s.

When winter was approaching, usually in September or October, the owner-manager, who had purchased the station with his wife's inheritance, left for Arizona to spend the winter months. The change in attitude on the part of the KFBB radio and TV staff was almost immediate. Sales increased, the sound of the radio station improved and the TV side showed a new professionalism. The assistant manager, who spent most of his time acquiring national business, let the two program directors keep the place running. And did it run! KFBB was the best place in Montana to work, until spring arrived.

Then it happened. Mister Manager returned. Nothing was right! The place looked and sounded horrible (in his estimation). Sales were not what they should have been, the announcers were not doing their job. The "Old Man's" first reaction was to fire at least three people, often the first ones who crossed his path, and put everyone else on probation. And, of course, the result was poor sales, bad ratings and a lack of motivation in the ranks. Employees quit in droves and the station suffered until fall.

At long last, Montana is seeing many of its own people enter broadcast work without having to relocate to an eastern or Pacific coast city to receive training and experience. Professionals are being attracted from out of state and those who have achieved a degree of excellence are being encouraged to stay.

The state will always have its share of stations operated by high school students and those who have been rejected by the larger markets. However, there is an increasing emphasis on hiring people for what they know and can accomplish rather than how low a salary they will accept. This is a step in the right direction, because as broadcast signals are imported from out-of-state by cable and satellite, local stations will need to offer programming that is comparable, or better than the imported "foreign fare."[133]

As in any industry, there will eventually be broadcast stations in Montana that will commit suicide on the rocks of the free enterprise system. At present, several Montana markets are over populated with broadcast services. Some may fail, and perhaps some should if they are not offering the services they were licensed to perform.

An alternative to failure is merger and consolidation. There are precedents for both in the merger of two Great Falls applicants in the 1940's, even before they signed on the air, along with the consolidation of two Butte stations in 1964.

In the years before 1990, an individual owner could only possess one AM and FM in a single market. Under new rules initiated in the final days of the Bush administration, many are taking advantage of new regulations that allow multiple ownership in a single market, based on its population. In many instances, stations in the same market are being operated by a single owner through Local Management agreements (LMAs).

In Billings, established AM/FM combinations have taken full advantage of these new duopoly rules. Citadel Communications Group (KDWG AM & KCTR-FM) purchased KZLS, changing it to KKBR (The Bear). Citadel also purchased KYBS at Livingston (now KATH) and switched frequencies with KBOZ-FM. Sunbrook Communications at Billings which already owned KBLG and KRKX recently purchased KYYA (FM). Sunbrook, which also operated KXTL and KQUY (FM) at Butte obtained KJLF and changed it to KAAR (FM). Missoula's KYSS/KLCY purchased KGVO in that city.

Common ownership of stations in separate cities may be an answer as well. A group of stations is easier to operate and has less overhead than several stations owned and managed separately. Both Sunbrook and Citadel have found this arrangement very profitable in Montana.

In the future, many other duopoly arrangements and LMAs will surely take place.

On the other hand, diversification may be preferable in the smaller markets where the only AM and FM facilities have a common ownership. A little competition can sometimes work wonders for any business.

In the past, Montana radio broadcasters have placed great emphasis on station "formats," with the essential ingredients being the type or style of music offered to the listener. Up to now, music has been of prime importance, along with the various methods of presenting or showcasing the songs. Other services, such as news, public affairs and special events have been relegated to secondary status.

In years to come, great emphasis will not only be placed on how the music is presented but also on what ingredients go along with it, such as news, features, weather, controversy and the promotion of public events. Radio will more and more become a forum for local opinion and discussion.

Adult listeners will look to radio more and more for information and less for entertainment. Even though new music forms may evolve, more people will look to tapes and compact discs for entertainment, thus allowing broadcasters to do the one thing they do better than any other medium, inform the listener.[134]

Listeners will expect radio to offer professional performers and a new accuracy in the reporting of news and local events. More talk formats will emerge, at least in the larger markets, along with all news stations, all prompted by the abundance of network service from the many satellite networks. In 1988, KBLG at Billings began the state's first "all-talk" format, utilizing programming from the Sun Radio network, Talknet and several

other services. Other stations, including KGVO and KMMS have followed suit.

The stations that become more state and local oriented will probably be
the most successful. Personalities will emerge with less and less emphasis
placed on the "non person" announcers. This will be especially true of
talk formats.

Educational FMs will continue to capture a share of listeners, while
Television will remain much the same, mostly controlled by the networks,
except for a few innovative local programs and newscasts.[135]

As determined at the beginning of this treastise, Montana broadcasters
and broadcasting have been different. Radio and TV in the state have
always been a challenge. Long may it remain that way!

There are no cut-and-dried answers to the problems of Montana broadcasters. Those engaged in this activity today will have to consider the pros
and cons of higher power, translators, interconnection, local orientation
and identity, professionalism, facility consolidation and formats that appeal
to the listener at every economic, political and educational level. Their
decisions will determine who will emerge as successful broadcasters in the
21st Century.

Signals from outside the state will vie for the listener's ear. However,
Montanans should not lose their access to the local microphone and
camera if Montana broadcasters are willing to compete and adapt as the
tastes and needs of their listeners change.[136]

Edmund B. "Ed" Craney, pictured on a photographic mural for the KXLF studios in Butte. The mural is now in possession of Greater Montana Foundation, Billings.

Courtesy of Ron Cass–KXLF

21

"There Was A Fellow By The Name Of Craney"

This section is a practically verbatim transcription of a tape cassette recording made by E. B. "Ed" Craney in 1986 in response to a request from a former employee who was working on a biographical sketch of Mr. Craney.

He graciously allowed me permission to use this material when he learned about this historical treatise.

The reason for the title applied to this section will become very obvious as the reader advances through the material.

Although I have attempted to transcribe the material on the recording exactly as Mr. Craney spoke it, in a few instances I have added a word or two in paranthesises in order to clarify the meaning or context of the statement made.

On occasion, the material was slightly rearranged when he digressed back to a previous statement. In a few instances, I deleted material that was not germane to the subject at hand or is covered elsewhere in this history. In every instance, I determined to retain the context at all costs.

While Mr. Craney was a major player in the history of Montana radio and television, we should be aware that there were many other persons, stations and events that shaped this history other than Craney, KGIR or the Z Bar Network. He was certainly not a "johnny-come-lately" in Montana broadcasting, but several stations antedated the advent of KGIR. No disrespect intended, "E.B!"

Go ahead, Ed! You're on.....

"It was 1921. I was going to school at North Central High in Spokane. I belonged to the radio club at the school and we used to talk to Doctor Shallenberger over at the school in Missoula, the University, as well as to a number of other hams.

"I had been going to North Central for a couple of years. I transferred over there from Flathead High School in Kalispell. I went there in the disastrous year of the flu epidemic and really lost half a year at that time.

All during the flu epidemic, I didn't have it, but right after the epidemic was over and schools reopened, I got it!

"In 1920 there was a sparsity of factory made (receivers) in the radio business. In Spokane there was one ham, a fellow by the name of Olson who worked for the Washington Water Power Company. He ran his ham set as a broadcast station for a couple of hours daily. This was the start of broadcasting in Spokane.

"I decided I wanted to graduate with the kids I started school with and needed 16 credits to do so. I was taking a scientific course in the school and had a chance to become advertising manager of the school news paper. I could earn a couple of journalism credits that way, but they didn't help me to graduate.

"I had taken typing in the Flathead High school, and the Journalism credit and the typing credit I made more use of them than any other subject I had been taking.

"I did want to become an electrical engineer and probably could have as my mother had saved $5,000 to educate me. In those days, I could have gone through college on the $5,000 without any trouble at all.

"As advertising manager of the paper, I was out after school hours soliciting ads all the time. This was the day of aviation. The war was over and aviation schools were abundant. A fellow by the name of Mister Messer had a school over on West First Avenue (Spokane) and I always sold him an ad, but he always wanted to talk.

"My time was valuable to me because I only had time to sell after school and Messer wanted to talk radio. Finally, he asked what I was going to do that summer, and I said I was going to try to get a job someplace, because I'd always worked in the woods, my father being a railroad and logging contractor. Right then he had a horse outfit (as) it was a pretty bad time for logging.

"Finally, one day, he told me that he and two other fellows were going to open up a radio store and wanted to know if I would work in it. I said, yes, and one day he gave me keys to Eight South Howard, which was in the Symons building. He told me to go down and check the stuff that was there and let me know what it was.

"It was an empty store. I checked in(to) the stuff and it was a bunch of Killburn and Clark radio equipment used on shipboard. I made a listing of it and told him what it was, mainly parts. As I have said, sets were almost non-existent.

"The store opened! I found out I was the manager. I was the only employee and I was the janitor also. Once in a while, a fellow with sort-of red hair would come in and look the place over and (then) go out.

"One day he asked me, 'If I buy these two fellows out, will you stay and run the thing?' And, I said, 'Well, I promised my mother I'd go to college this year!'

He was Tom Symons.

He said, "Oh, I've gone through college and I think you're in a new business and you should stick with it! You should grow up with it! There are going to be all kinds of chances to make a good living in this."

I said, "Mister Symons, we need a broadcast station in this town."

He said, "Can you build one?"

I said, "Yes, I believe I can, but I've got to go over and get a First Class license in order to run the thing!"

He asked if I could do that.

I said, "There's a YMCA radio school in Seattle and with two weeks there, I think I can get a license."

"Well," he said, "Why don't you go over and get it?"

"But," I said, "I told my mother I'd go to college. Will you talk to her?" He said, "yes!"

So, I got my mother down to the store and Tom talked to her.

She said, "Times are tough in our business and I'll let the boy stay and work for a year!"

The year never quit! That was the only job I ever had......!

I got my First Class License and we got the station on the air. It was my old ham set (transmitter) with a few more dollars spent on it. It was five watts of power. It covered the city of Spokane out to (the town of) Sprague, Washington, 18 miles to the southwest.

KXLY (then KFDC) went on the air October 18, 1922. The Dorr-Mitchell Company had a station there, but it had closed. And, the Pacific Telephone and Telegraph Company had a station there and it closed. So, KXLY (KFDC) is the pioneer station that still remains in Spokane (see footnote #29).

The radio business was not very good. I made some sets up. some regenerative sets, which infringed on Major Armstrong's patents, there's no question about that! I later met Major Armstrong back in Washington (DC). He was the inventor of the regenerative set (receiver), the superheterodyne and FM (Frequency Modulation).

Our big trouble at the time of the building of the transmitter was (how) to modulate it, to impinge on the radio wave the voice wave.

The first transmitter I built had an absorption loop antenna and we put the voice on it through a transformer in the antenna circuit. I guess we got one or two percent modulation. The first change that came about was a system that gave us about ten-percent. I think that was a development of RCA.

In those days, 1922, we could talk to each other on the broadcast field (band) after midnight. That's when the distant listener was developed. They called themselves "DXers." You had cards printed up and you would send everybody who wrote you a DX card, either verifying they were correct or telling them they were "all wet!"

We used to talk with CFCN in Calgary, an amateur by the name of Mr. Moore in Walla Walla and a fellow, I forget his name, at Telegraph Hill in San Francisco. We tried rebroadcasting each other and completed that successfully. You'd be on the air almost every night, late, and you'd broadcast during the evening hours.

(In) the election of 1924, we carried (results) off the ticker tape of a firm known as Lousier and Wollcott. The front page of the newspaper had not yet been destroyed (by radio). It took Franklin Delano Roosevelt with his magic words to do that! That was to come almost ten years later.

Let's talk about other improvements made by these late broadcasts: Phonograph records were made by talking into a megaphone, or singing into it. Then it would vibrate a little cutting needle and record in beeswax. Then the "mud" plates were pressed out of that. Phonograph records were pretty bad. To broadcast them, we had just a plain telephone microphone and we stuck that in the opening of a Sonora phonograph.

I ran the store, a radio supply company, made up sets, which we sold, and ran the station as well as the experimental work. I was a good janitor and not really much of anything else. I got a lot of my ideas from W. W. Grant who had the CFCN, Calgary station.

The engineers worked hard on improving microphones. A different group of engineers worked hard on improving modulation. The engineers working on microphones came up with a condenser-type microphone. First, they came up with a microphone that had four carbon buttons on it. You connected it with a battery just as you did the phone company (microphone) with a single button. There were those who thought the four button one was a lot better.

We didn't have cathode ray tubes in those days, the oscilloscope had not been invented, so it was impossible to tell what was happening. (Maybe) we only thought it was better!

When the condenser microphones came out, that was definitely better. We bought a Jenkins and Adair microphone first and an RCA second. That was because Jenkins and Adair hit the market first.

The phonograph companies got in on the condenser microphone before they got to us and it was a race to see who could get the best quality out first. The phonograph companies usually got the best quality first and the stations second. They went back and forth many times on the quality of recording that was available.

The engineers working on modulation greatly improved it, modulating the whole envelope of the signal, with about 120 percent. Improvements were made in the tubes (we) used. When we finally got a five kilowatt transmitter, it had water cooled tubes in it. Today, water cooled tubes are no more. They have made tremendous progress in the equipment that is now available. RCA, which was the standard to go by, is no longer making that equipment.

The programming of radio started out with just a sponsorship. The Willard Battery Company had an hour show and all they did was announce that, "This show is brought to you by Willard Batteries." Kraft Cheese did the same, as did cigarette advertising.

Senator Dill wrote the Radio Act of 1927 and the Communications Act of 1934. He said he worked hard on these bills, mainly because of me! He said I was all over the dial with the station there in Spokane, and Senator Dill lived in Spokane. He was a great friend in later years. Congressman White of Maine co-sponsored the bill in the House.

I got into the wholesale radio business and traveled out into the field, selling. I got to Butte, Montana in 1927 and discovered they did not have a radio station. In 1927, the mines were all running in Butte and it was quite a town. I put in an application for Butte and it was granted in 1928.

On my first visit there, I had gone to Morris Weiss, manager of the Finlen Hotel and told him I was going to build a radio station there and could I put it on his roof. He said that would be fine! I did not bother Morris Weiss between that time and when the grant was made in 1928.

KGIR were the call letters assigned to the Butte station and it went on the air January 31, 1929. The equipment was in Montana and I went to see Morris Weiss to tell him it was there and that I could start building right away.

He told me, "I'm sorry, Craney, I can't let you go there. We can't have a station on this building!"

Knowing what I do now of Butte, I should have been suspicious right away, but I was totally inexperienced in Butte politics.

My next job was to go out and try to find a place near the Finlen Hotel where I could place the station. For the granting of the station you have to give the exact location of where the station is going to be. I ended up with Carl Shiner of Shiner's Furniture Store, which was across the street and down half a block from the Hotel.

Well, the equipment got out on the sidewalk and I came into the store one day (when) the carpenters were just about finished upstairs. Carl met me and said, "I'm terribly sorry, Ed, but you're not going to be able to have the station here!"

I said, "For God's sake, what's the trouble?"

He said, "Do you know Carlos Ryan?"

Carlos Ryan was the son of J.D. Ryan, who was president or chairman of the board of the Anaconda Company back in New York. Somewhere in the back of my mind I remembered that Tom Symons had taught the chief engineer, the chief geologist of the Anaconda Company's son how to fly. He married a Spokane gal and they had some kids that Tom taught to fly. So, I called Tom in Spokane and told him we were having trouble.

He said, "What kind of trouble?"

And, I said, "I've been with Carl Shiner. We are not allowed to go on the Finlen Hotel. Now, they're blocking us from going on the Shiner's Building. Can you call your friend and tell him to tell J.D. Ryan that we're not too bad of people? I've been with his son and his son wants to know whether we're going to let the Union speak or not. I told him, yes, that we were, and that we would also let the Anaconda Company. We'll run the thing just like the sidewalk is run outside your building there."

That wasn't what the son wanted to hear! He wanted to let them (the Company) walk on the 'sidewalk and keep all the Union people off!"

Tom said, "I don't know whether these fellows are in New York, or down in Chile. He spends a lot of time in Chile."

I said, "I know, but take a chance!"

Tom called, and got him and we got permission to open the station from the Anaconda Company. That was our first brush (with Butte politics). The next came in 1937 when I got off the train in Butte at noon from New York. I had left my salesman, Leo McMullen, in charge of the station. McMullen had been a hoisting engineer for 17 years on the hill. Then he ran the Butte Ice Company (and worked) for the bank where his brother-in-law was cashier. Then he came to work for us.

He met me and said, "We're 'unfair' with the Miners Union and they are going around town knocking all of our accounts off!"

I said, "How in the H--- can they do that?"

He said, "Well, MacPherson (an announcer) ad libbed a title to a news story. I don't know what he said, but he says he said, "Here's a man among men." They say he said, "Here's a man that's a man!"

The news item was about the mayor of Syracuse, New York, refusing to aid strikers. The (Butte) Miner's Union was out on strike against the Company at the time.

I said, "Have you talked to the Miner's Union?"

He said, "I haven't talked with anybody,"

"Well," I said, "Let's go home and I'll take these bags home and we'll see what can be done!"

I called the secretary of the Union. I used to know his name, but I can't remember it. He later went down to Denver."

I told him, I said, "You're just breeding a scab on your nose. I don't see how you can declare us unfair, when you won't talk to me! I could go on the air and refute what was said, no matter what it was! And, I would be happy to do that, but you didn't give me a chance!"

He said, "Would you meet with our committee?"

I said, "Sure, I'll meet with anybody!"

So, he sent the committee around that had been going around knocking our advertisers off, and I talked with them. I was still unfair! So, I called them again and told them what the situation was and we went all over the thing (again)!

Then, he said, "Will you meet with our Central Committee?"

I said, "I told you I'd meet with anybody I could!"

The Central Committee was about 50 members.

He said, "I'll get the Central Committee together. You'll have to come over here!"

I said, "I'll come over there."

They had a little platform (set up) and a little table and a chair up on the platform and they put me there. They all wanted to talk at once.

I said, "Now wait just a minute!"

I repeated the same story I had told the secretary to begin with.

And I said, "Now, I don't have an awful lot of money, but I can run the station for a little while. But don't ever think you're going to be any better off than you are with me running it, because I'll put it up for sale and the Anaconda Company will buy it, because I could have sold the station the morning after we opened to either Clark or the Company. But, I kept it and ran it myself. You don't have enough money to buy this station and you're better off where you can talk and they can talk, than to get it like the Anaconda Standard is now, because you can't get in there for anything. They'll run the station the same way they run the newspaper. You're better off with me running the thing."

I went out of the meeting and walked back to the station. I got there and the phone was ringing. It was somebody from the sixth floor of the Hennessy Building, the Anaconda Company's Offices.

They wanted to know why I told the miners they could broadcast.

I said, "I've told you and I've told them that you both can Broadcast. That's the way it is while I'm running the station."

The Miners decided I was still unfair. In those days we had a line going to Western Union, so I could ring a bell at Western Union and they would send a person over for your message.

I rang the bell and sat down and wrote out an announcement to tune in at seven o'clock that night. There was going to be a broadcast on the air pertaining to KGIR being fair with the Miner's Union. I wrote out what I was going to say. It was just a story of what had taken place since I had gotten off the train.

It included the call I had from the Anaconda Company and I gave it to the messenger and told him to take it over to the Miner's Union. I was soon fair with the Miner's Union. They just couldn't afford to let it be known that the Company had spies in their meeting, and those spies were on the Central Committee. They (miners) didn't know who they were. I had no further trouble with the Anaconda Company or the Miner's Union after that!

How did we get NBC? RCA had a fellow by the name of "Scoop" Russell working for them. He liked to play poker and we played poker on a train from Detroit to Washington, D.C. most of one night. He wanted to know how well I knew my Senators. Well, I didn't know either one of them. Tom Walsh was the senior senator and B.K. Wheeler was the junior senator.

They had sent a fellow by the name of Fritz Marancy out to Butte to get me to join the National Association of Broadcasters. I joined and we were the only station in the state of Montana that was a member. They then proceeded to have a fellow by the name of Evans (who was) with Westinghouse, resign and had me appointed to fill his vacancy.

They thought Wheeler was either going to be chairman of the Interstate Commerce Commission or Vice President with Roosevelt. They wanted someway to obligate Wheeler to them.

I had sent wires to the Kiwanis and the Rotary Club, Chambers of Commerce, people like that, to get telegrams back (to me) if they wanted NBC in Butte. Tom Walsh had taken these telegrams and gone up to NBC, which was then at 711 Madison Avenue.

It wasn't Tom Walsh they wanted anything to do with. They wanted Wheeler! I went to Wheeler's office. He was in Europe, coming back the next day. The first two times I met Wheeler were in his office and he never remembered either one of them. The first time I met him alone, the second time I had Tom Symons with me, but he never remembered either one of them!

He thought the Anaconda Company owned some part of the station, and he was death against that, as he had an experience with the newspapers in which he found out the Anaconda owned them, and he thought the same thing had happened with the radio.

I asked the Senator when he was going to New York. He said he did not have any idea when he was going to New York, and I told him that NBC was thinking of putting us on their network, but they wanted to have him have his say on it.

He said, "You mean they want me to ask them to put you on?"

I said, "Well, I suppose that is what it is all about. I had the service clubs write you about it."

"Yeah," he said, "But you didn't have any labor unions."

I said, "I didn't think of that."

"Well," he said, "You'll have to start thinking of them in Butte!"

Scoop Russell told me to get (with) the fellow from the Billings station, bach there, and I got Charlie Campbell from KGHL in Billings to come back. Scoop got Wheeler to go up to New York. He was in with M.H. "Deak" Aylesworth, president of NBC. Wheeler asked where we were and Deak said, "Let them cool their heels a while longer."

That was the way we got on NBC. Wheeler never did ask (him) to put us on (NBC). Deak would have one fellow come in, he'd ask him a question and we were supposed to be on with KOA and KSL. KSL was at that time NBC and we were supposed to get all the programs they got. That isn't the way it worked! We had 15 minutes of time available for NBC programming on Wednesday night and that was all! They never did put us on with KSL and KOA.

Then, they had a fellow by the name of Fillman come to Butte after the election when they knew Wheeler wasn't a candidate for Vice President. When they weren't able to sell Montana stations on the programs they had thought they were going to sell, he tried to take the lines out.

I had seen how important it was to have political influence. By that time I had ingratiated myself to Wheeler and it worked out Okay. He kept the lines running by just calling NBC and saying, "Lou, you've established yourself there. How can you call yourself a national network if you're not in there (Montana)? You'll have to say, "We're a national network with everything except Montana! Go ahead and do that!"

And, so we kept the network into Montana.

Several years later, Columbia (CBS) came into Montana in Great Falls and Missoula. A fellow by the name of Harry Butcher was the Washington, D.C. vice president of CBS and ran the station there. He was the Naval to Eisenhower all during his stay in Europe. Harry was a good bridge player. That's how he got the job!

Harry came out and spent two weeks with me and Wheeler in Great Falls and spent about 30 minutes with him while he gave a talk putting the two Montana stations on the CBS network and that was that.

(More Technical Material)

One of the other problems in early-day radio was the whine of the generator. You had to have 3,000 volts to run the tubes at that time. A generator had to have a filter system on it to take the hum out. As I said before, in the early days, we didn't have any tubes that (could) have a picture on them (an oscilloscope) of what the sine wave looked like in any part of the gear. You experimented around and tried to get rid of the hum as best you could.

Willard (wet cell) batteries were the great thing of that day. They made a tray of batteries which gave you 24 volts and these were pint-sized batteries. The thing we did in Spokane was to get 6,000 volts of Willard batteries. We had DC current in Spokane and 220 volts were available in the downtown area. All you had to do was connect up your batteries with a switch that put them in parallel (to charge) or in series when you were broadcasting. We had two sets, which when connected in series gave you 3,000 volts and when connected in parallel could be charged with the 220 volts available. That gave you a good, clear signal.

A mercury vapor arc gives you a good signal with 3,000 volts very easily. These arcs were used by movie houses to attract attention out on the street. We used one of those in Butte and we used a generator in Butte. We had a great deal of trouble with the hum from the generator. In Butte, by the 1930s, we were getting into factory-built equipment with various filters on it that cleared up the hum completely.

The experimentation that we had done in the earlier period when I was in Spokane, paid off. Television did not go through the same (on the air) experimental period that radio went through.

(Television)

CBS had a motor driven (color) system that they not only tried to force on the public, the Commission ordered it used! RCA had a different system, the one we have today, and it is an obsolete syetem, too. The rest of the world uses 625 lines for a picture, where(as) the U-S uses 525 (lines). You have to make those pictures compatible with the international use of television today.

France uses 800 and some lines, Britain uses the 625 lines on their UHF signals but a lesser number on VHF. Test gear was the answer in the television field and the engineers knew a great deal more about (the) signals and how to clean the hum out of them and how to break them up into a millionth part of a second. That's one thing RCA did when they got to the stage to have test gear that could tell you what was happening. That was the difference between radio development and television development.

(Recording)

During the war (WWII) the Germans developed a wire recorder. On a very thin piece of wire they recorded information. And, when we found them, we brought them over to this country and that was the start of the tape recording industry. It was much easier to record on tape than on a wire which was continually breaking.

RCA and Ampex were running a race to see who could make a recorder for television. Bing Crosby was backing the Ampex deal. I was down in his office and out in front of it he had a picture of an airplane going across the sky. Like a darn fool, I didn't think it was too practical. I could have made some money then, and I could have made some money later on, when I saw it demonstrated at an RCA meeting. But, when you're living so close to the thing, sometimes you just miss out!

(Music)

In 1932 a fellow by the name of Claude Mills was with ASCAP and he called a meeting of broadcasters into Chicago. He told us that he thought we knew something about broadcasting, but he was going to teach us something that afternoon. He proceeded to tell us that we were going to pay a five-percent ASCAP fee. Five percent (of our net) was a lot of money! ASCAP had a $25,000 (per year) flat fee for NBC and CBS, and they wanted those networks to force all the stations on the network to have an ASCAP license, or not give them any program service.

It was a great challenge, and I got into the ASCAP fight right up to my ears. A fellow by the name of Gene Buck was the head of ASCAP. We had a County Attorney by the name of Edward Dussault in Missoula. He determined that Gene Buck was in Phoenix, Arizona and had him arrested because there was a law in Montana that allowed for the licensing of any (musical) number that was filed in the state. ASCAP paid no attention to it. They didn't file any (of their) numbers and we were protesting that we wanted their numbers on file so we would not play them. This raised all H--- with ASCAP and with Buck privately.

I took all the records that we had and tried to determine what numbers were ASCAP and what other numbers could be played. We took all of the ASCAP numbers out of the file and it didn't leave much!

Century Publishing Company had mainly public domain numbers and it was picked up by BMI, Broadcast Music Incorporated, an organization that broadcasters put together. I was in on that fight, because I would not join with the other broadcasters.

A fellow by the name of Johnny Gillman of WOW in Omaha, Nebraska and I wanted the transcription companies to clear the music at the source and tell us who owned the various numbers they recorded. Finally a fellow by the name of Clauber, a vice president of CBS got up at the meeting.

He said, "We're only going to play this one way. We're going to play it our way. And, you can take it or leave it!"

The broadcasters had to buckle down into Clauber's hands. I had Wheeler meet with the networks, and finally he told me to get Buck into his office and tell him he could bring his lawyer with him and I was going to be there and I could have a lawyer with me. I took the secretary, who was a lawyer of the broadcaster's association with me to that meeting. Wheeler, at first, was very much on Buck's side. At noon, a knock came at his outside door, and he went to see who was there. A senator wanted to buy him lunch.

He (Wheeler) came back in and said, "Gene, you're not as popular here as you used to be!"

That was the first break we had.

Gene said, "Well, why not Senator?"

Wheeler said, "That was a senator wanting to take me to lunch, and I told him who was in here, and he told me to keep my hands over my pockets."

It was Chan Gurnee of Nebraska that went by. I found out later that Chan was in the broadcast business at Yankton, South Dakota (WNAX).

Wheeler said, "Gene, why don't you go up there to your friends on Madison Avenue and get them to pay you for the music they use?"

Gene said, "we do that! They each pay us $25,000."

The Senator said, "Well, that's nothing. You want these stations to pay you the big part of what the networks should be paying you. You're up there where you can go and collect fees from them. Go do that!"

That was clearance at the source (CS).

He said, "When you want to collect on news out in Montana, you don't own that news, Gene. Why don't you just collect on the music that you own?"

Gene said, "We have no way to keep track of it!"

Wheeler said, "Let the stations keep track of it for you. They can be just as honest keeping track of the music that they play, as they are now paying you on the money they take in."

That was payment for what you used. Wheeler went to three different attorney generals to keep a law suit that the networks had started with ASCAP and they had agreed to have it folded, but Wheeler kept the thing alive! It was the suit that finally settled the ASCAP problem.

The government decreed payment for what you used along with clearance at the source, and that's what we wanted all the time.

(Formats)

Today, everybody has a "type" of station; a western station, a rock and roll station, an all talk station. Barry Goldwater (was) the head of the radio-television section of the Interests Commerce Committee of the Senate. If Barry Goldwater would (have) questioned some of the "truck" that is on radio and Television, we would clear it up and make it much better that it is today! They call that censorship. I call it good broadcasting! And I think that if the Commission would set some broadcast licenses for a hearing at renewal time, you'd soon get out of such hearings what was considered good broadcasting! It would give a yardstick to follow and certainly you'd have no dirty movies on television today!

(Super Power and Clear Channels)

When the law (Communications Act) was written, there were 40 clear channels that had only one station on them. (Senator) Dill tried to get all the channels duplicated, but was unable to do so. The Clear Channel group of stations were making about fifty cents on every dollar they took in as profit, and they had a pretty strong lobby going in Washington.

He (Dill) did get the clear channels reduced to twenty-five. They experimentally put 500,000 watts on WLW in Cincinnati. This effected stations as far away as Wheeling, West Virginia (where) a station was about to lose its network affiliation.

Any six stations, properly spaced in the country, could cover the nation day and night with this much power. That was what the networks wanted. They desired to control the stations that covered the entire country. Sarnoff at RCA had Scoop Russell working on it all the time.

Wheeler was chairman of the Senate Commerce Committee. He finally called chairman McNinch of the Communications Commission up to his office in 1938. McNinch had been in the power commission, if I remember right, before taking chairmanship of the Communications Commission. Wheeler talked to him about the fact that he didn't want to see the struggle for dominance that had been taking place in the power industry (happen) in the broadcast field, and he didn't think McNinch wanted it either.

McNinch promised to start a hearing on the Clear Channel thing. In 1938, hearings were started. I talked to Roy Ayres, who was then the governor of Montana, about going to Washington and testifying as to what "super power" would mean in Montana. He agreed to do it, but when the hearings started, he said he couldn't do it, but would appoint John Claxton, my attorney, to represent the state of Montana. So, I took Claxton to Washington and he opened the hearings.

If they were going to have "super power" stations, then of course, Montana wanted one, because that was the rural part of the United States that needed that kind of coverage. (However) there was no town in Montana that could support a super-power station (in) those days.

Today, there are no totally "clear" channels with one station (on) the frequency. They finally have them all duplicated, and that brings a lot of service to a lot of areas that wouldn't have it otherwise!

They sent chairman Fly of the Commission to sell (Wheeler) on the idea of giving six 750,000 (watt) stations to each one of the three networks.

I happened to be there in Washington when Fly came up for lunch to see Wheeler and talk to him about it. That was shot down in a hurry!

Fly was a good commissioner, except that he was sold ideas by a very professional and persuasive salesman, Scoop Russell. Russell was more influential in radio law than any other one (person) in the country. He did a great job for Sarnoff, but the clear channel thing was settled by commission decisions after I got out of the business.

(Programming)

Let's talk about programming. It was extremely hard to get programs into isolated areas such as Montana. They finally made 16 inch discs which they called transcriptions. They were syndicated around (the state) in place of a network connection.

Amos 'n Andy was a program that was funny, but could not be seen or heard today, because of the change in thinking by the population about black people. They were two white guys that put on a nightly show on the networks. They started on transcription and soon got a network contract. They were about the first transcriptions to be made.

There was a fellow by the name of Tom Brennan over in Bellingham, Washington, who put on a similar program to Amos 'n Andy, taking all the parts in the program himself.

A fellow by the name of MacGregor, down in California, had a program called "Cecil and Sally." The Chicago Tribune had a program called "Louie's Hungry Five." That was a little German band!

We bought all these programs for Montana with the right to resell and circulate them around the state. And, we did just that!

Ed Krebsbach (KGCX) was up in Wolf Point next to the Assiniboine reservation and there was no way he could pay enough to satisfy the owners of the program to send them to him, but I could get a transcription into Butte, reship it to him and have him "bicycle" it on to somebody else. We would come out all right on the program costs that way.

Those 16 inch discs, at the time World War II started, were on aluminum. They soon had to change over to glass, one-quarter plate glass, which was coated with acetate on both sides. That was our tape recorder of the day.

We handled political speeches in the same way. We had a cutting head and would get a speaker into Butte's studio and cut a 15-minute program, and then we shipped it around to various stations.

All of these (discs) had a high hissing sound in the background which was the cutter (head) cutting down through the acetate. It wasn't until after the German wire recorder came out (and) with the refinements in

American that developed into tape recordings, that we had the means of recording a program and playing it back satisfactorily.

(Musicians Union)

One thing you might be interested in knowing about was the musicians union. A fellow by the name of Petrillo, who was manager of the city's parks in Chicago, was the head of the musicians union. He wanted every station to hire a band and use it as station property. It takes a good income to support a band of musicians, particularly in the days of the "Big Bands." He was successful in that he stirred up the Commission which made you announce (it) when you played a phonograph record!

Petrillo had a girl friend who worked for NBC. He would take her around the country (with him). It was quite a deal! The car that he drove around in had bullet-proof glass in it!

In the ASCAP fight, a lawyer by the name of Ken Davis was on our side. I was in Chicago with him and we went to see Petrillo. He sent us his car, the bullet-proof one, around to the various parks that he had beautified. He told his chauffeur where to take us and we went out and rode around in the car. As I remember, it was a big, black Cadillac.

(Miscellaneous)

We had the "Night Owl" program at KGIR in which we sent out membership cards out all over the country. It was on Saturday night and (for) anybody who wrote in, we'd send (them) one of the Night Owl cards. We used to get a lot of mail, from a lot of states, all over the country!

KGIR was the only non-directional (at night) regional station in Montana. T.A.M. Craven, who later became a commissioner on the Radio Commission, was the engineer who devised directional antennas. With directional antennas you could put stations closer together and direct their signals away from each other and thus make better use of the frequency you're assigned to broadcast on.

In the early days of radio, the Commissioners were mainly radio people. There was a fellow by the name of Bellows who was with the CBS station in Saint Paul. He became a commissioner. You could go in and talk with Bellows and get a lot of information on how to run a radio station. He was a very, very fine fellow with a lot of savvy and would give you information you couldn't get any other place.

Some automation equipment came out. I was trying to think of the fellow that had it. He had been an NBC page boy and he came through Butte on his way to Canada to sell his gear. It was mainly tape recorders with an automated timing device. You could set that up to run all day!

We were down on South Montana (Avenue) when he came through and we bought from him an automated "job" that worked quite well. It would be 'way behind times today. We were in the TV business at the time we bought it and radio was relegated to automation, when possible.

The first TV station I had was in Spokane. It was the second station on the air over there (KXLY), the first being the newspaper-owned station (KHQ) which blocked us from (initially) getting on Mount Spokane, which was a logical place to put a TV station in that area. KXLY (TV) has many listeners up in Canada because of that location.

Speaking of KXLY, at the end of the war (WWII), the Commission went ahead and granted all kinds of stations. I saw that call letters were not going to mean anything, unless you could get a whole group of them (that were similar).

In 1941, we bought KXL in Portland. Tom (Symons) was down there running it when he died in October of '41. When the war ended, I decided that the "XL" call (sign) should be promoted as a single station. That is when we got our calls changed to "XL."

Spokane was KFPY and that became KXLY. Butte became KXLF; Bozeman. KXLQ; Great Falls, KXLK; Missoula KXLL (and Helena KXLJ). We had a station in Ellensburg that was KCOW and became KXLE. We sold them as the "XL" stations and that worked out very well!

22

Paul Harvey In Montana

For years, rumors persisted that the renown Paul Harvey of ABC Radio fame had worked in Broadcasting in Montana early in his career. Most of the tales centered around KGVO.

On August 31, 1987, the author heard Harvey's noon newscast in which he referred to his radio days in Missoula.

The following letters, along with an attached treatise by Mr. Harvey should settle the matter once and for all.

PAUL HARVEY DID WORK IN MONTANA!!!

KKMT RADIO
710 P.O. Box 710, Ennis MT 59729
(406) 682-7171

1 September 1987

Paul Harvey
ABC Radio
360 North Michigan
Chicago IL 60601

Dear Mr. Harvey,

You could have knocked me down with a feather, or over with a noodle during your broadcast of yesterday, August 31st. You were creating some fond memories of your early radio days when you mentioned you worked in MISSOULA! Since there is only one Missoula in the U-S-A, there could be no doubt you were talking about Missoula, Montana, and because of the time frame, radio station KGVO!

This has a double interest to me! I am in the process of assembling a book ("Voices in the Big Sky") that hopefully documents the history of Montana broadcasting. I am aware that Chet Huntley was an alumnus of Montana, but was not sure about Paul Harvey. I also had the pleasure of working at KGVO On two different occasions, once for the colorful A.J. Mosby and again for the equally illustrious Dale G. Moore,

Paul, if you could take a moment to give me some dates as to when you were in Missoula, along with a few memories of those days, it would add some real interest to the manuscript. I realize you are the second busiest man in the world, next to the president, but if you could TAKE A FEW MOMENTS TO ASSIST ME, I'd appreciate it!

I believe John Rolfson also worked at KGVO in the late 1940s. He went on to be with ABC in Paris. Also, Pat Connell, the first black man to be hired as a staff announcer for a major network came from Montana and KGVO. He went to CBS!

Hope you carry through with Paul Junior's suggestion about the book!!

Thanks for any help you can offer!

Howard McDonald
President and General Manager
KKMT

September 23, 1987

Mr. Howard McDonald
President & General Manager
KKMT Radio
P. O. Box 710
Ennis, Montana 59729

Good Morning, Howard McDonald ...

It was before WWII that Angel and I
stretched our Missoula honeymoon into
two happy years at KGVO. We lived
on University Avenue in "dear
Apartment 8" and the daily walks to
work were such a joy.

Art Mosby and his family remained
friends for the rest of his years.

Every good wish,

PH:jw
PAUL HARVEY NEWS
360 North Michigan Avenue
Chicago, Illinois 60601

P.S. Attached is something I wrote
on the occasion of Art Mosby's birthday
11-16-68. If appropriate for your purpose,
help yourself.

Art Mosby's Birthday

Recorded by Paul Harvey October 12, 1968 - Art Mosby's birthday.

It's a beautiful day in Missoula today!
Good evening, Americans.
This is Paul Harvey — Aurandt.

Oh how I did want to be with you to help the "boss" celebrate this day. But I have been committed for more than a year to a speaking engagement in Chicago tonight which I just could not set aside.

A recorded message is a poor substitute for a personal reunion, but I had to do what I could to add my congratulations — and just for a moment — to reminisce.

Boss, do you ever tell the story of my first football broadcast? Anybody but you would have chased me out of Missoula and maybe out of the industry after that disastrous bluff.

And remember the time I threw the union organizer downstairs and almost got you in a peck of legal trouble.

My, you did have to be forgiving in those days. And perhaps, learning how to from you, I have managed to forgive a few impetuous, impulsive young fellows in the years since.

I recall the first time we met the first thing I said: "Well, Mr. Mosby, we drove straight through from St. Louis but we got here ahead of the blizzard !" And you tilted your head and squinched up your eyes and asked, "What blizzard?"

I, like so many, had the idea that Montana gets helplessly snowed in from Thanksgiving to Easter.

And in the months that followed — honeymooning in dear Apartment eight .. out on University ... Wasn't the lovely landlady's name "Kelly"? The apartment with the bald-headed hill in the backyard and our old car parked alongside. The white Nash Lafayette that's enshrined yet on our Ozarks farm.

No, Angel and I recall Missoula — the walks to work — the river — the man-on-the-street broadcasts — and you — so frequently. No memories of our life together are more special. Some ways I was richer on 29 dollars a week in Missoula than anywhere else anytime since.

And I'll never forget how during the insecure years afterward when Angel and I were rookies in the Big League ... A note from you once in a while included a gracious vote of confidence and a reminder that we were always welcome home in Missoula. That wherever I was ... it was always a beautiful day in Missoula. I derived more self-confidence from your standing by than you can possibly realize.

So, "Boss," your kindness to Paul Aurandt had very much to do with shaping the career of Paul Harvey. I hope it may be pleasing to you as your manyfold success has delighted and continued to inspire me.

I did not mean to run on this long. I just meant to say "Happy Birthday." And to offer a firm and meaningful handclasp across the miles until hopefully sometime soon I can deliver that handclasp in person.

Keep a light in the window.
For Paul Harvey Aurandt —
Goodnight.

23

Chet Huntley

Next to movie actor Gary Cooper, Montana's most famous native son would have to be newsman Chet Huntley.

Chester "Chet" Huntley was born in Cardwell, Montana, a small community east of Whitehall, where his father worked for the Northern Pacific railroad as a telegrapher. The year was 1911. In 1913 his family moved to the area around Saco, in northeastern Montana, to settle on land that had been opened to homesteading.

When the dry years of the 1920s created "dust bowl" conditions in the once fruitful area, Huntley's father returned to work with the Northern Pacific at Willow Creek. Later, Chet's father held positions with the N-P at Whitehall, Norris, Pony and Bozeman.[138]

Because of his abilities in writing and debate, he earned an academic scholarship to Montana State College in Bozeman in 1929. The same abilities brought him a similar grant in 1933 to the Cornish School of Arts in Seattle. There he began his broadcasting career at KPCB as announcer, writer and janitor.

Following graduation from the University of Washington at Seattle, Chet went to KHQ in Spokane and in 1937 transferred to KGW, Portland. By 1939 he was at KFI, NBC in Los Angeles and later moved on to KNX (CBS) in the same city. By 1943 he was on the special events staff at KNX and was producing and voicing a ten minute news and commentary feature on the Pacific Coast CBS stations.[139]

During his stay in Los Angeles, Chet often spoke out concerning the lack of Black Americans in Broadcasting, especially on dramatic programs. When Pillsbury Flour balked at sponsoring a program featuring blacks cast in roles that were outside the normal stereotypes that were common on radio at the time, Chet offered an opinion that sponsor sensitivity to blacks in normal roles also accounted for the lack of news coverage of events in the black community.

He was reported as saying, "I presume that the reason for less Negro news was due to sales resistance. Sponsors would probably fear boycott of their products." In 1944, Huntley produced an award-winning series,

"These Are Americans," on KNX that also dealt with blacks in the military as well as broadcasting.[140]

Chet's next move was to NBC New York as a news reporter and writer. In 1956 he was teamed with David Brinkley to report the election returns on NBC. This resulted in the "Huntley-Brinkley Report," one of the top rated news programs of the 1960s and '70s. Huntley also did occasional news and commentary features for NBC Radio.

Following retirement in 1971, he and his wife, Tippy, returned to Montana to build the Big Sky Resort south of Bozeman. He passed away soon afterward and is buried in Bozeman's Sunset Hills Cemetery.

It had been rumored that he would seek either the Montana governorship or a seat in the U-S Senate had death not intervened.

Huntley is the only broadcaster to be enshrined in the Montana Hall of Fame at the State Capitol building in Helena, and was the first to be inducted into the Montana Broadcasters Association Hall of Fame.

Tippy ventured into Montana politics and went on to marry TV actor William Conrad.

24

A Chronology Of Montana Broadcasting

1919   Charles Ashley Dixon broadcasts music and talk from his home near Stevensville.

1922   KDYS, Montana's first licensed station begins broadcasting on May 17 from the offices of the Great Falls Tribune. In October, F.A. Buttrey begins KFBB in his store at Havre. KFCH begins on November 7 under sponsorship of the Billings Gazette. An educational license is issued the same day to KFED at Billings Polytechnic Institute. KFDO operating at Bozeman. KFCH ceased broadcasting on December 10.

1923   Montana's first "remote" broadcast, the Dempsey-Gibbons prize fight was broadcast on both KFBB and KDYS from Shelby on the Fourth of July. KDYS ceased broadcasting sometime in the fall. An unlicensed station broadcasting at Missoula with numerous other clandestine operations on the air across the state.

1925   KUOM at Missoula begins on February 17 from the University of Montana campus on 1230 kHz with 250 watts.

1926   KGCX begins occasional broadcasts on October 5 from the First State Bank at Vida.

1927   March 21, KGEZ opens at Kalispell with a basketball broadcast.

1928   June 8, Charles Campbell starts KGHL at Billings, using the slogan, "The Northwestern Auto Supply Company Station." The first day of broadcasting features a remote broadcast from the governor's office in Helena. On September 24, KUOM broadcasts a speech by presidential candidate Al Smith.

1929   F.A. Buttrey moves KFBB from Havre to Great Falls. January 21 E.B. Craney opens KGIR at Butte. August 21, KGCX moved to Wolf Point and power increased. October 31, KUOM ceases broadcasting and license is allowed to expire. Missoula without radio service.

1931	On January 17, KGVO begins broadcasting from studios in the Union Block (later Radio Central Building) in Missoula.
1936	KFBB increases power to 5,000 watts and joins the Columbia Broadcasting System. KGVO affiliates with CBS the same day.
1937	KPFA begins at Helena on October 1st. KGIR and KPFA form the Z Bar Network. KGIR moves to Nissler Junction and increases power to 5,000 watts. White's Radio Log lists KGIR as being "near" Butte, Montana.
1939	October 15, KRBM opens at Bozeman and becomes the third station in the Z Bar Net.
1941	KRJF (1340) begins at Miles City on September 4th. World War II puts a freeze on any new stations or expansion.
1946	On September 8th, KBMY (1240), Billings' second radio station and Montana's first post-war station begins. KANA (1230), Anaconda November 6th, featuring a part-time hook-up with KGVO. KGCX and KRJF join Mutual (MBS).
1947	Montana's post-war radio boom begins as new stations sign-on the air: KPRK (1340), Livingston, January 10th; KBOW (1490), Butte on February 14th; KXLK (1400), Great Falls (fourth station of the Z Net; KXLO (1230), Lewistown on June 24th; KIYI (1230), Shelby on August 4th and KXLL (1450), Missoula (fifth station of the Z Bar): KOJM (730), Havre begins October 31st followed by KAVR (1340) a few weeks later in the same city.
1948	Three new stations in Montana: KMON (560), Great Falls starts on May 30th; KOPR (550), Butte, June 9th and KXGN (1400) at Glasgow on September 23rd.
1949	KBMN (1230), Bozeman begins September 14th and KFDW (1340), Helena in October. 1950 Palatial downtown studios of KGVO burn on February 10th. KLCB (1230), Libby starts December 23rd.
1951	Fairmont Corporation, a subsidiary of the Anaconda Company, attempts to purchase KFBB. A flood of protest follows. Fairmont seeks dismissal of the application to purchase. KOOK (970), Billings, begins March 20th with 5,000 watts and brings CBS to Eastern Montana.
1953	KXLF-TV (Ch.6), Montana's first TV station begins at Butte on August 14th, followed by KOPR-TV (Ch.4) on August 28th. KOOK-TV (Ch.2) begins in Billings on November 9th.
1954	KFBB-TV (Ch.5), Great Falls starts March 21st. KGVO-TV (Ch.13), Missoula opens July first. KLTZ (1240), Glasgow on the air August 14th. KOPR-TV closes September 20th.

1955	This year sees four new radio stations in Montana:KBTK (1340), Missoula on July 15th; KOYN (910), Billings, September 25th; KBGF (1450), Great Falls, September 23rd and KOFI (930) Kalispell on November 11th.
1956	No new station start-ups.
1957	KDBM (800), Dillon begins January first; KVCK (1450), Wolf Point on September first and KXGN-TV (Ch.5), Glendive on November first.
1958	KXLJ-TV (Ch.12) on the air in Helena January first. KGHL-TV (Ch.8), Billings, March 19th and KRTV (Ch.3), Great Falls on October 5th.
1959	Three new radio stations: KGVW (630), Belgrade February first; KYSS (910), Missoula, June 27th and KURL (730), Billings, October 15th.
1961	KLYQ (980) begins on February third at Hamilton and KRBN (1450), Red Lodge on December 7th.
1962	KPWD (FM) (100.1), Plentywood, Montana's first FM station signs on June first. KGLE (590), Glendive begins August 22nd and KHDN (1230), Hardin on December 29th.
1963	KGVW-FM (96.7), Belgrade starts November first; KDRG (1400), Deer Lodge on October 31st; KURL-FM (97.1), Billings opens December 17th and KARR-FM (106.1), Great Falls' first FM signs on with a New Years Eve broadcast.
1964	KFLN (960), Baker starts July 14th; On August 16th, KBOW and KOPR at Butte merge, taking the KBOW call sign and the KOPR 550 frequency. KARR-FM becomes KOPR (FM).
1965	KUFM (89.1), goes on the air January 31st from the University of Montana at Missoula; KSEN, Shelby increases power to 5,000 watts on 1150 kHz.
1966	In December, KGLT at Montana State in Bozeman begins as the state's second "educational" FM on 91.9 mHz. MSU students had been operating a campus-limited carrier-current station with the unauthorized call signs KATS and KRAP. KOFI, Kalispell becomes Montana's first 10,000 watt AM on 1180 kHz, a clear channel that had been reserved for WHAM at Rochester, New York. KOFI later increases to 50,000 watts, another Montana first.
1967	KWYS (920), West Yellowstone begins December 20th, carrying some programming from KXXL at Bozeman. West Yellowstone is the smallest community in the nation with a radio station.
1968	KCFW (TV) (Ch.9) begins on June 10th at Kalispell.

1969	Five new stations in Montana; KLYQ-FM (95.9), Hamilton on February 11th; KOYN-FM (93.3), Billings, April 5th; KYSS-FM (94.9), Missoula May 11th; KYUS (TV) (Ch.3), Miles City on August 29th and KIVE (FM) (96.5), companion to KGLE, Glendive on December 21st.
1970	KTVM (Ch.6), Butte opens as a full-time repeater of KGVO-TV, Missoula on May 21st and KPAX (TV) (Ch.8) starts in Missoula as a repeater to KXLF-TV on June 5th.
1971	KCGM (FM) (95.7) begins at Scobey on June 21st; KHTC (FM) of Helena Vo-Tec Center begins broadcasts sometime during the year.
1972	KANR (FM) (98.9), Great Falls, second FM station starts June 19th; KDBM-FM (98.3) signs on August first. KNUW (FM) (94.5), sister to KMON, Great Falls begins the first of October; KBOW-FM (94.1), Butte starts October 26th and KMSM (FM) (91.3), Butte begins intermittent broadcasts on November 22nd.
1973	KEMC (FM) (91.7), Billings, voice of Eastern Montana College, gets underway on April 25th.
1974	KGLM (FM) (97.7), Anaconda starts January 18th; At Missoula, KYLT-FM (100.1) begins on July 29th and KALS (FM) (97.1), Christian-oriented station at Kalispell starts November 15th.
1975	These stations begin in the state: KPQX (FM) (95.9), Havre on March 8th; KLCM (FM) (95.9), Lewistown, April first; KRWS (FM) (95.3), Hardin (date unknown): KCAP-FM (101.1), Helena; KIKC (1250), Forsyth, October 10th and 5,000 watt KBOZ (1090) in Bozeman December 19th.
1976	Two new stations in Montana; KERR (1070), Polson opens on March 22nd and KMTX (950), Helena on November first.
1977	KRER (FM), low-power NCE station at Billings Career Center starts in March. At Missoula, KDXT (FM) (93.3) opens on April 29th and KYBS (FM) (97.5), Livingston starts in December. The downtown studios of KSEN in downtown Shelby burn on November 17th.
1978	KBMS (FM) (98.5), companion to KGHL, Billings begins on August 14th; KZIN (FM) (96.3) starts as companion of KSEN December 9th; KOPR (FM), Great Falls, becomes KOOZ (FM) and KBOW-FM is changed to KOPR (FM), returning the call sign to Butte.
1979	Six new stations in Montana: KJJR (880), Whitefish on February 14th; KOOK-FM (102.9), Billings on August 14th; KATQ (1070), Plentywood opens September 18th as AM companion

to KPWD (FM); KLYC (1490), Laurel has a September start; KBLL-FM (99.5) signs on in November and KTXX (1450), Whitefish, December 6th.

1980   KQUY (FM) (95.5), Butte starts February 7th; KMMR (FM) (100.1), Malta September 9th; KXXE (FM) (101.3) begins as companion of KIKC, Forsyth; KOUS (TV) (Ch.4) starts at Hardin on November 26th and KNOG (FM) (90.1) at Northern Montana College at Havre on April first.

1981   KGCH (FM) (93.1), Sidney starts as adjunct to KGCX; KYYZ (FM) (92.3) begins as co-station to KVCK at Wolf Point September first; KQRR (FM) (92.3), starts at Ronan October 4th and KSDY (FM) (95.1) as Sidney's second FM November 2nd.

1982   KLFM (FM) (92.9) begins in Great Falls February 14th under the management of KBOZ's Bill Reier.

1983   KLAN (FM) (95.5), Glasgow on March first; Christian-oriented KXEI (FM) (96.1), Havre signs on July 28th; KCTB (FM) (102.7), Cut Bank, November first; KRYK (FM) (101.3), Chinook on November 19th; and KFXZ (FM) (98.5) starts at Kalispell September 12th. On September 21st, KYSS (AM) changes city of license to East Missoula in order to obtain night time operation.

1984   KMCM (FM) (92.5), Miles City opens on November 8th and KGPR (FM) (89.9) starts in Great Falls as repeater for KUFM, Missoula. Montana's first educational TV station, KUSM, begins at Bozeman. In December, most of Montana's Class IV (local AM) stations commence 1,000 watt night time operation.

1985   KMTX-FM (105.3) begins at Helena on January 15th and KUEZ (FM) (102.5) starts at Missoula January first.

1986   KUUB (FM) (95.1) Bozeman starts on August 14th; KTNY (FM) (101.7) comes on at Libby April 5th; KMTA (1050), Miles City (Kinsey) starts in October and KTGF (TV) (Ch.16), Montana's first UHF station starts up at Great Falls on September 21st.

1987   KDRF (FM) (96.7) companion to KDRG, Deer Lodge, begins January first. Later in the year, KDRG and KDRF are off the air due to problems with the IRS and SBA. KSKR, Whitefish is sold by the SBA. December 6th, KOHZ (FM) (103.7) opens at Billings as "Cozy."

1988   On January first, most Montana daytime-only stations are given low-power night time authority by the FCC. KJLF (FM) (92.7), Butte's Christian station begins on October first. KECC (FM) (90.7) begins as adjunct to Custer Community College at Miles

City; KHKR (680), East Helena has a May 26th start and KOFI-FM (103.9), Kalispell opens on June 10th.

1989   KAFM (FM) (99.5), Red Lodge starts in early summer with low power operation only to leave the air soon after. KHKR-FM (104.1) starts April 13th and KRXX (FM) (104.1) begins in July with call sign KFBA.

1990   No new stations. KANA leaves the air; KBSR (KFBN) at Laurel is on and off the air. KKUL, Hardin is off for extended periods.

1991   KTMF (TV) (Ch.23) starts on UHF November 16th at Missoula. KANA makes several abortive attempts to resume a regular schedule.

1993   KZLO (FM) (99.9) begins at Bozeman, operated by Reier Broadcasting. Reier buys silent KBMN; KVCM (FM) (103.1) starts at Helena as repeater for KXEI, Havre; KAFM, Red Lodge returns as KMXE (FM).

1994   KRSQ (FM) (101.7), licensed to Laurel begins on June 9th.

At this writing, several Montana stations are off the air and there are no announced plans for their return. KSDY at Sidney left the air in 1989. In the fall of 1993, the FCC terminated their authority and deleted the call letters. KSKR at Whitefish suffered a similar fate. KCTB, Cut Bank had its license revoked in 1993 because of inactivity. KRBN at Red Lodge is off the air and probably will not return. KGCX at Sidney, along with its FM companion, KGCH, reportedly left the air in 1994 and no date of return has been forthcoming.

KHTC (FM), a non-commercial educational entity, operated by the Helena Vo-Tec Center has been gone for several years, along with KRER (FM), an endeavor of the Career Institute in Billings. Channel four KOUS (TV) at Hardin is dark.

Every effort had been made to assure the accuracy of this station chronology. Many dates were taken from the Broadcasting/Cable-casting Yearbook. Supplemental information was gleaned from newspapers, station files and other documents, such as the Richards' Thesis. Much personal knowledge of several individuals, including the author, was also utilized.

The author has been on hand for the inaugural broadcasts of several Montana stations, including KBMN, KOPR (AM), KMON, KRTV, KBOZ, KBZN (FM), KOHZ (FM) and KUUB (FM). He was there, receiver tuned to the station frequency, waiting for the carrier to come on for the very first day of broadcasting. In the case of KBOZ, he was in the studio, waiting to read a newscast.

25

"Voices In The Big Sky!"

Broadcasting Hall Of Fame[137]

ASHLEY C. DIXON	Stevensville banker who operated a clandestine station in the Bitterroot area, circa 1919. Dixon was probably Montana's first unofficial "broadcaster."
FRANK A. BUTTREY	Founder of KFBB at Havre, which was later moved to Great Falls.
O.S. WARDEN	Owner/manager of the Great Falls Tribune, circa 1922. Founder of KDYS, Montana's first licensed station.
EDMUND B. "ED" CRANEY	Founder of Butte's first radio station (KGIR, Montana's first radio network (The Z Bar Net); Montana's first TV station (KXLF-TV) and Skyline, Montana's first TV network.
CHARLES CAMPBELL	Founder of KGHL at Billings and owner of the Northwestern Auto Supply Company.
DR. G. D. SHALLENBERGER	Manager and engineer for KUOM, the state's first educational station at the University of Montana at Missoula.
ED KREBSBACH	Montana Banker and founder of KGCX a station located at Vida, Wolf Point and Sidney.
ARTHUR J. "ART" MOSBY	Western Montana broadcast pioneer. Founder of KGVO, KGVO-TV (KMSO) and KANA. Also, real estate developer (Farviews).
DONALD TRELOAR	Pioneer announcer and manager for KGEZ. Treloar kept the station in his home for several years.

JEFF KIICHLI — KGHL pioneer. First radio engineer in the state to become manager of a commercial radio station.

ANTHONY "TONY" LOPUCH — Innovative engineer for KFBB Radio and TV. Spent later years at KULR (TV).

FRED "FRITZ" BARTLETT — Long-time engineer for KGHL/KIDX, Also master story teller.

W. C. "BUD" BLANCHETTE — Announcer for KGVO, National Sales manager for KFBB Radio and TV. Executive for KGVO and Western Broadcasting Company.

WILLIAM "BILL" STROTHMAN — Popular KGVO and KXLL morning announcer (1940s and 50s). Co-founder of KBTK (Missoula). First host and originator of the "Highlander Tavern on Z Bar.

MARION DIXON — Announcer, salesman, sales manager for KGVO. Co-founder of KBTK. Also in real estate.

HARRY TURNER — Pioneer announcer for KGHL, also orchestra leader. Turner's voice was very similar to that of Brace Beamer (The Lone Ranger).

MAURY WHITE — Long-time morning and sports announcer for KGHL. Also worked at KFBK, Sacramento.

ARNIE ANZJON — Manager, KGIR (KXLF), host of the "Montana Booster" program on the Z Bar Net.

ERNEST "ERNIE" NEATH — Pioneer Montana station manager and salesman for KRBM (KXLQ). Accomplished musician.

DON WESTON — Award winning newsman, sportscaster for KGVO. Political commentator.

JOSEPH "JOE" SAMPLE — Owner/operator of KOOK radio and TV and the Montana Television Newtork. Director, Greater Montana Foundation.

JACK PROVIS — Innovative engineer for KGIR and the Z Bar Network. He was also a craftsman.

ED COONEY — Butte announcer and first manager for the original KOPR. Former SESAC representative.

PAT GOODOVER — Announcer/manager for KRBM, KXLL and KXLK (KARR). State senator from Great Falls.

K. O. MACPHERSON — Manager, KXLK, KOOK, KCAP and other state stations. KOOK was named in his honor.

ARTHUR "ART" WEBER — Radio and TV personality for KGVO and KFBB. Great Falls businessman.

RONALD "RON" CASS	Announcer/sportscaster who became manager of KXLF-TV. Known for the Jerry Lewis Telethons and July 4th parade in Butte.
DAN SNYDER	Announcer, manager, salesman for KGVO, KBMN. Founder of KBGF and KRTV. Former manager for KZMT/KCAP and KGHL/KIDX.
CATO BUTLER	Longtime Helena newsman. Colorful sports reporter. Worked with KCAP/KZMT. The "Dean of Montana newscasters."
DAN MILLER	Billings morning personality, KOOK and KUUS. Former manager KBIT/KOOK and KOHZ (FM). Known as "Major Dan, the morning man."
DONNA KELLEY HOFFMAN	Announcer, KBMN; news anchor, KXLY-TV, Spokane, Co-anchor, CNN & Headline News, Atlanta.
WILLIAM "BILL" REIER	Owner/founder, KBOZ, KBOZ-FM (KBZN), KLFM, KOHZ and KZLO. One time manager of KOOK.
JACK BOGUT	Montana DJ personality of KDBM and KBMN. Host of KGHL's "Bogue's Gallery." Became well known on KALL, Salt Lake City and KDKA, Pittsburgh.
STAN STEVENS	Manager/co-owner, KOJM/KPQX and Havre cable system. Montana governor 1988 to 1992.
CONRAD BURNS	Founder of Montana's Northern Ag-Net and KLYC. Farm circuit lecturer. Elected to U-S Senate 1988, re-elected in 1994.
CHET HUNTLEY	NBC newsman, founder of Big Sky Resort. Only broadcaster in Montana State Hall of Fame.
PAUL HARVEY	Famous ABC Network news commentator. Worked at KGVO prior to World War II.
PAT "THE CAT" CONNELL	Announcer/DJ for KGVO and Negro Broadcasting System. First black to be hired by a major network (CBS).
RONALD P. "PAX" RICHARDS	Announcer, KGVO; Newsman for KGVO, KFBB, and KREM, Spokane. Faculty, School of Journalism, University of Montana. Co-founder, KMTX. Former assistant to Senator John Melcher.

DONALD "DON" BRADLEY   Program Director/announcer, KGVO. Station manager for KTVQ: Owner/manager KTVG and KMON AM/FM.

These have also contributed to Montana Broadcasting:

Dean Alexander	Norma Ashby	Hugh Bader
Terry Bass	Benny Bee	Lonnie Bell
Jim Bender	Larry Binfet	Jerry Black
Charlotte Brader	Taylor Brown	Steve Campbell
Reed Collins	Paul Crane	Earl Crowder
Ken Davis	Luin "Dex" Dexter	Al Donahue
Paul Van Ehlis	Leo Ellingson	Ian Elliott
Harold Erickson	Cliff Ewing	Gene Fennamore
Joy Fanning	Joe Flaherty	Jim Goodrich
Bob Greer	Paul Hatton	Merlin Hedin
Dale Heidner	Bill Holter	Stan Hooper
Dean Jansma	Rich Jessen	Al Johnson
Leonard Kehl	Warren Kemper	Gus Koernig
Dick Kober	Jay Kohn	Ed Kohlman
Keith Krebsbach	Fred Lark	Bob Lasich
Pat Lee	Bob Leinweber	Glen Lockwood
John Lyons	Ted Mangun	Jim Manning
Don McDonald	Bill Merrick	Stan Meyer
Shag Miller	Vic Miller	Don Moe
Dick Monaco	Dale Moore	Chet Murphy
Wilbur Myhre	Dorthea Neath	Cy (R.L. Martin) Noe
R. J. "Bob" Nelson	Burt Oliphant	Don Oliver
Al Ortmann	George Oschli	George Ostrom
Chad Parrish	W. H. Patterson	Ed. Peiss
Norm Penwell	Gary Peterson	Gene Peterson
Hal Phelps	Wes Pidcock	Kim Potter
George Reardon	Larry Roberts	Tom Robischon
John Rolfson	Chuck Scofield	John Severson
Paul Simitzes	Dick Smiley	Virginia Smith
Homer Stenerson	Ray Styles	Cy Taylon
Roger Torrenga	Jerry Tyo	Vonnie Vaughn
Ron "Fat Jack" Warner	Jack Womack	Bill Yeager
Ed Yocum	Joe Zahler	Bill Zaputil

Certainly, there are others who have not been noted by the author-CHM!

26

Montana Broadcast Stations

City	Station	Frequency
Anaconda	KANA	580 kHz
	KGLM	97.7 mHz
Baker	KFLN	960 kHz
Belgrade	KGVW	640 kHz
	KSCY	96.7 mHz
Billings	KBKO	103.7 mHz
	KBLG	910 kHz
	KCTR-FM	102.9 mHz
	KDWG	970 kHz
	*KEMC	91.7 mHz
	KGHL	790 kHz
	KIDX	98.5 mHz
	KKBR	97.1 mHz
	KMAY	1240 kHz
	KRKK	94.1 mHz
	KURL	730 kHz
	KYYA	93.3 mHz
Bozeman	KATH	93.7 mHz
	*KBMC	102.1 mHz
	KBOZ	1090 kHz
	*KGLT	91.9 mHz
	KMMS	1450 kHz
	KMMS-FM	95.1 mHz
	KOBB	1230 kHz
	KZLO	99.9 mHz
Butte	KAAR	92.7 mHz
	KBOW	550 kHz
	*KMSM	106.9 mHz

	KOPR	94.1 mHz
	KQUY	95.5 mHz
	KXTL	1370 kHz
Chinook	KRYK	101.3 mHz
Columbia Falls	KCWX	95.9 mHz
Deer Lodge	KDRG	1400 kHz
Dillon	KDBM	1490 kHz
	KDBM-FM	98.3 mHz
East Helena	KHKR	680 kHz
	KHKR-FM	104.1 mHz
East Missoula	KLCY	930 kHz
Fort Belknap Agency	KAEP	88.1 mHz
Forsyth	KIKC	1250 kHz
	KIKC-FM	101.3 mHz
Glasgow	KLAN	93.5 mHz
	KLTZ	1240 kHz
Glendive	KDZN	96.5 mHz
	KGLE	590 kHz
	KXGN	1400 kHz
Great Falls	KAAK	98.9 mHz
	*KABS	91.9 mHz
	KEIN	1310 kHz
	*KGPR	89.9 mHz
	KLFM	92.9 mHz
	KMON	560 kHz
	KMON-FM	94.5 mHz
	KMSL	1450 kHz
	KQDI-FM	106.1 mHz
	KXGF	1400 kHz
Hamilton	KBMG	95.9 mHz
	KLYQ	1240 kHz
Hardin	KKUL	1230 kHz
Hardin-Billings	KBMJ	95.5 mHz
Havre	*KNMC	90.1 mHz
	KOJM	610 kHz
	KPQX	92.5 mHz
	*KXEI	95.1 mHz
Helena	KBLL	1240 kHz
	KBLL-FM	99.5 mHz
	KCAP	1340 kHz
	KMTX	950 kHz
	KMTX-FM	105.3 mHz
	KVCM	103.1 mHz

	KZMT	101.1 mHz
Kalispell	KALS	97.1 mHz
	KBBZ	98.5 mHz
	KDBR	106.3 mHz
	KGEZ	600 kHz
	KOFI	1180 kHz
	KOFI-FM	103.9 mHz
Laurel	KBSR	1490 kHz
	KRSQ	101.7 mHz
Lewistown	KLCM	95.9 mHz
	KXLO	1230 kHz
Libby	KLCB	1230 kHz
	KTNY	101.7 mHz
Livingston	KBOZ-FM	97.5 mHz
	KPRK	1340 kHz
Malta	KMMR	100.1 mHz
Miles City	KATL	770 kHz
	*KECC	90.7 mHz
	KMCM	92.5 mHz
	KMTA	1050 kHz
Missoula	KDXT	93.3 mHz
	KGRZ	1450 kHz
	KGVO	1290 kHz
	KMSO	102.5 mHz
	*KUFM	89.1 mHz
	KYLT	1340 kHz
	KYSS	94.9 mHz
	KZOQ	100.1 mHz
Plentywood	KATQ	1070 kHz
	KATQ-FM	100.1 mHz
Polson	KERR	750 kHz
Red Lodge	KMXE	99.5 mHz
Ronan	KQRK	92.3 mHz
Scobey	KCGM	95.7 mHz
Shelby	KSEN	1150 kHz
	KZIN	96.3 mHz
Sidney	KGCH	93.1 mHz
	KGCX	1480 kHz
West Yellowstone	KWYS	920 kHz
Whitefish	KJJR	880 kHz
Wolf Point	KVCK	1450 kHz
	KVCK-FM	92.7 mHz

* = educational station   (CP) = construction permit

+MONTANA TV STATIONS+

CITY	STATION	CHANNEL	
Billings	KTVQ	2	
	KSVI	6	
	KULR	8	
Bozeman	KCTZ	7	
	*KUSM	9	
Butte	KTVM	6	
	KWYB	18	(CP)
	KXLF-TV	4	
Glendive	KXGN-TV	5	
Great Falls	KFBB	5	
	KRTV	3	
	KTGF	16	
Hardin	KOUS	4	(1)
Helena	KHBB	10	
	KTVH	12	
Kalispell	KCFW	9	
Miles City	KYUS	3	
Missoula	KECI	13	
	KPAX	8	
	KTMF	23	
	*KUFM-TV	11	

* = educational station
(1) Off air, status unknown

+THE MONTANA BROADCAST SPECTRUM+

kHz	call	city
550	KBOW	Butte
560	KMON	Great Falls
580	KANA	Anaconda
590	KGLE	Glendive
600	KGEZ	Kalispell
610	KOJM	Havre
640	KGVW	Belgrade
680	KHKR	East Helena
730	KURL	Billings
750	KERR	Polson
770	KATL	Miles City
790	KGHL	Billings
880	KJJR	Whitefish
910	KBLG	Billings
920	KWYS	West Yellowstone
930	KLCY	East Missoula
950	KMTX	Helena
960	KFLN	Baker
970	KDWG	Billings
1050	KMTA	Miles City
1070	KATQ	Plentywood
1090	KBOZ	Bozeman
1150	KSEN	Shelby
1180	KOFI	Kalispell
1230	KKUL	Hardin
1230	KLCB	Libby
	KXLO	Lewistown
	KOBB	Bozeman
1240	KBLL	Helena
	KLTZ	Glasgow
	KLYQ	Hamilton
	KMAY	Billings
1250	KIKC	Forsyth
1290	KGVO	Missoula
1310	KEIN	Great Falls
1340	KCAP	Helena
	KPRK	Livingston
	KYLT	Missoula
1370	KXTL	Butte

1400	KDRG	Deer Lodge
	KXGN	Glendive
	KXGF	Great Falls
1450	KGRZ	Missoula
	KMMS	Bozeman
	KMSL	Great Falls
	KVCK	Wolf Point
1490	KBSR	Laurel
	KDBM	Dillon

mHz		
88.1	*KAEP (CP)	Ft. Belknap
89.1	*KUFM	Missoula
89.9	*KGPR	Great Falls
	* app	Kalispell
90.1	*KNMC	Havre
90.7	*KECC	Miles City
91.3	* app	Butte
	* app	Missoula
91.7	*KEMC	Billings
	* app	Helena
91.9	*KABS (CP)	Great Falls
	* app	Hamilton
	*KGLT	Bozeman
92.3	KQRK	Ronan
92.5	KMCM	Miles City
	KPQX	Havre
92.7	KAAR	Butte
	KVCK-FM	Wolf Point
92.9	KLFM	Great Falls
93.1	open	Sidney
93.3	KDXT	Missoula
	KYYA	Billings
93.5	KLAN	Glasgow
93.7	KATH	Bozeman
	open	Conrad
94.1	KOPR	Butte
94.1	KRKX	Billings
94.5	KMON-FM	Great Falls
94.9	KYSS	Missoula
95.1	KMMS-FM	Bozeman
	*KXEI	Havre
	open	Sidney

95.5	KBMJ	Hardin-Billings
	KQUY	Butte
95.7	KCGM	Scobey
95.9	KCWX	Columbia Falls
	KBMG	Hamilton
	KLCM	Lewistown
96.3	KZIN	Shelby
96.5	KDZN	Glendive
	app	West Yellowstone
96.7	KSCY	Belgrade
	open	Deer Lodge
97.1	KALS	Kalispell
	KKBR	Billings
97.5	KBOZ-FM	Livingston
97.7	KGLM	Anaconda
97.9	open	Shelby
98.3	KDBM-FM	Dillon
98.5	KBBZ	Kalispell
	KIDX	Billings
98.7	app	Ennis
98.9	KAAK	Great Falls
99.5	KMXE	Red Lodge
	KBLL-FM	Helena
99.9	KZLO	Bozeman
100.1	KATQ-FM	Plentywood
	KMMR	Malta
	KZOQ	Missoula
100.3	open	Great Falls
100.5	app	Baker
100.7	app	Livingston
101.1	KZMT	Helena
101.3	KRYK	Chinook
	KIKC-FM	Forsyth
101.7	KTNY	Libby
	KRSQ	Laural
102.1	*KBMC	Bozeman
102.5	KMSO	Missoula
102.7	app	Cut Bank
102.9	KCTR-FM	Billings
103.1	*KVCM	Helena
103.5	app	Bozeman
103.7	KBKO	Billings

103.9	KOFI-FM	Kalispell
104.1	KHKR-FM	East Helena
104.9	app	Cascade
105.3	KMTX-FM	Helena
105.7	open	Outlook
106.1	KQDI	Great Falls
106.3	KDBR	Kalispell
106.9	*KMSM	Butte
107.3	open	Great Falls

Permits for these stations have been cancelled by the FCC:

1490	KMCW	Great Falls
100.3	KOOZ	Great Falls
107.3	KFTC	Great Falls

app= application
(CP)= construction permit

CHANNEL	call	city
2	KTVQ	Billings
	open	Anaconda
3	KRTV	Great Falls
	KYUS	Miles City
4	KOUS(1)	Hardin
	KXLF-TV	Butte
5	KFBB	Great Falls
	KXGN-TV	Glendive
6	KTVM	Butte
	KSVI	Billings
	*open	Miles City
7	KCTZ	Bozeman
8	KPAX	Missoula
	KULR	Billings
9	KCFW	Kalispell
	open	Havre
	*KUSM	Bozeman
10	KHBB (CP)	Helena
	open	Miles City
11	*KUFM-TV (CP)	Missoula
	open	Havre
12	KTVH	Helena

13	KECI	Missoula
13	open	Glendive
	(CP)	Lewistown
14	open	Billings
	*open	Dillon
	open	Cut Bank
16	KTGF	Great Falls
	*open	Glendive
17	open	Wolf Point
18	KWYB (CP)	Butte
	*open	Havre
20	KVME (CP)	Billings
23	KTMF	Missoula
24	open	Butte
26	open	Great Falls
32	*open	Great Falls

(1) = Off the air, status unknown
app = application
CP = construction permit
* = educational channel

27

Glossary Of Terms

Amplitude Modulation (AM). A system of broadcasting in which the information is transmitted through variations in the amplitude of the carrier wave.

Call letters or call sign. The particular designation given a radio or TV station by the FCC. Most broadcast call signs begin with "W" east of the Mississippi River and with "K" west of the Mississippi, although there are several exceptions. Some older stations may have three letters, but most stations have four. No two stations may have the same call letters, but an FM or TV affiliate of an AM station may use that station's call sign with an FM or TV suffix.

Clandestine. When applied to broadcasting, a station that operates without governmental authorization and usually from a secret location.

Clear Channel. A radio frequency in the AM band that is occupied by only one station, or in some cases, only one station at night. There are no clear channels remaining in the United States. All US clear channels have been broken up with smaller stations allowed on the fringe areas of the dominant station.

ERP. Effective Radiated Power. The power of a radio or TV station may be increased by using a special antenna that increases the coverage area of the station without increasing the power output of the transmitter.

Federal Communications Commission (FCC). The agency of the United States government that regulates all forms of broadcasting; radio and TV as well as Cable TV, special services such as amateur stations along with telephone and short wave. In radio's early days, communications was regulated by Department of Commerce and the Federal Radio Commission.

Frequency modulation (FM). The system of broadcasting in which the information or intelligence is transmitted by variations in the frequency of the carrier wave. FM has better fidelity than AM and is practically static free.

Ham. An amateur radio operator. Hams are assigned to certain bands or frequencies and may transmit voice or code between individual stations.

Kilohertz (kHz). A term signifying 1,000 hertz (or cycles per second). The kilohertz was at one time known as the kilocycle (kc).

Megahertz (mHz). A term signifying one million hertz (or cycles per second). The megahertz was at one time known as the megacycle (mc).

Network. Two or more radio or TV stations hooked together in order to broadcast common programming. Network programs are normally sent to individual stations by satellite.

Pseudonym. A false name used by a radio or TV broadcaster, sometimes known as an "air name." Montana broadcaster Harold Butzloff used the pseudonym of "Benny Bee."

Regenerative Receiver. A radio receiving set that uses the electronic phenomenon known as "regeneration," where the signal is fed back through the amplifying tubes many times in order to accomplish high amplification.

Satellator. An FM translator that is programmed from a satellite rather than rebroadcasting a nearby station. Satellators can only be used by educational FM stations to rebroadcast their signals. James "Jim" Goodrich of the Moody Broadcasting Network is credited with the idea as well as the terminology.

Sideband. A portion of an FM station's carrier frequency that can be used to transmit supplementary information which will not be detected by a normal FM receiver. Special adapters or receivers are required. Sidebands can be used to carry additional programming or data such as technical information, paging or facsimile. Also known as an SCA.

Superheterodyne Receiver. A radio or TV receiver that uses the principle where the various incoming signals are converted to a common intermediate (IF) frequency. This simplifies amplification and the conversion of the radio signals to audio.

Syndication. A method of producing radio and TV programs and distributing them apart from the facilities of a network. Old-time radio programs were syndicated through acetate discs and later on audio tape. Most radio syndications today are on tape or Compact Discs. TV syndicators use video tape or satellite feeds.

Translator. A low-power FM or TV transmitter that rebroadcasts the parent station's signal beyond its normal range or coverage area. The rebroadcast signal is "translated" onto a frequency different than that of the originating station.

+FOOTNOTES+

[1] Personal correspondence with William Lang. editor, "*Montana, the Magazine of Western History*", dated February 1, 1985.

[2] Richards, Ron(ald) P., "*A History of Radio Broadcasting in Montana*," master's thesis, University of Montana, Missoula 1963.

[3] Brier, Warren J. and Blumberg, Nathan B., (editors) *A Century of Montana Journalism*, Mountain Press, Missoula, Montana, 1971.

[4] Malone, Michael P. and Roeder, Richard B., *Montana, a History of Two Centuries*, University of Washington Press (Seattle), 1977, page 282.

[5] *Broadcasting/Cablecasting Yearbook*, Broadcasting Magazine, Washington, D.C., various editions.

[6] *Broadcast Station Pioneers*, T.H. White, Compuserve Services, (Broadcast Forum), 1/1/92, no pagination.

[7] Richards, op. cit., page 11.

[8] "Radio at the Old Alma Mater," George Riggins, author, *Radio World Magazine*, November 8, 1989, page 26.

[9] Richards, pages 11-12.

[10] Frost, S.E., *Education's Own Stations*, Chicago 1937, page 34.

[11] "*It Happened in Montana*," Historical cartoon by artist Jim Masterson, from the Greater Montana Foundation Collection, Museum of the Rockies, Bozeman, Montana. Courtesy of Museum of the Rockies (1995). KFDO may have operated out of the Cosner Hotel in downtown Bozeman.

[12] Personal conversation with "Uncle" Lyman B. Walton, circa 1950. The call sign KBOZ is now used by a leading Bozeman station.

[13] *Great Falls Tribune*, May 20, 1922, cited by Richards thesis.

[14] ibid, November 25, 1923.

[15] Brier and Blumberg, page 25.

[16] *Wolf Point Herald*, April 16, 1929, cited by Richards.

[17] Richards, op. cit., page 25.

[18] "*Stay Tuned*," Sterling, Christopher H., and Kittross, John M., Wadsworth Publishing Company, Belmont, California, 1978, page 110.

[19] Richards, pages 35.51.

[20] ibid., pages 51 to 63.

[21] "*Empire of the Air*," Lewis, Thomas. Harper Collins Publishers, New York, 1991, page 229.

[22] Brier and Blumberg, pages 80-81.

[23] Richards, pages 70-71.

[24] ibid, pages 73-85.

[25] "*History of KGHL*," Unpublished manuscript, furnished to the author by Richard Kober, former station manager for KGHL, August 1965.

Presumed to be lost during management change. When KGHL began, 100 watts was considered "super power."

[26] The excellent ground conductivity in Central Montana and the Dakotas coupled with KGHL's ⅝th wavelength antenna made this coverage possible.

[27] "Two Babes Grow Up," *Montana Standard*, Butte, Montana, Sunday March 11, 1979.

[28] ibid.

[29] "Wheeling and Dealings Dot Road Trod by Radio," *Montana Standard*, Butte, Montana, Sunday March 11, 1979. This was from Craney's own testimony. Two stations antedated KFDC. KFZ operated in Spokane from 3/23/22 until 9/8/23 and KOE began on 4/12/22 and closed on 10/7/22. KFIO also began before KFDC. See footnote #6.

[30] "KGIR, Blast of Sound Heard 'Round the Town," *Montana Standard*, Butte, Montana, Sunday March 11, 1979, page 17.

[31] ibid.

[32] Both Anaconda and the Montana Power Company wanted control of the station as they controlled most of the State's newspapers.

[33] "KGIR, Blast of Sound," op.cit.

[34] *Butte Daily Post*, February 1, 1929.

[35] *Butte Daily Post*, January 4, 1929.

[36] "KGIR, Blast of Sound."

[37] ibid

[38] The person furnishing this information has requested he not be identified as long as he lives.

[39] Personal experience of the author while employed by the Z Bar Net at KXLQ, Bozeman.

[40] Personal interview with Tom Jenkins corporate engineer for Craney in the early days of KGIR. March 1986 when employed by KUSM (TV), Bozeman.

[41] Richards, page 106.

[42] ibid.

[43] Richards, page 107.

[44] ibid.

[45] "KGVO Moves," paid supplement to the Sunday Magazine of the *Sunday Missoulian*, Missoula, Montana, February 2, 1981.

[46] Richards, page 64. Mosby had problems with this location. It had formerly been the site of a well-known Missoula brothel.

[47] "Fire Destroys KGVO Plant," *Daily Missoulian*, February 29, 1950.

[48] Personal interview with Dan Snyder, former manager of KCAP/KZMT, Helena, Montana, September 6, 1986.

[49] Richards, pages 99-100.

[50] Personal remembrances of the author who resided in the Bozeman area during these years. KRBM kept a tight schedule during the war years.

[51] Richards, page 114.

[52] For many years, various radio listening guides listed this station as KPJF. This was an error, evidently perpetuated by one guide copying another. See "*White's Radio Log*," Summer 1950, page 28.

[53] "High Powered Radio Opposed by Montana Broadcasters," *Great Falls Tribune*, March 9, 1948, page 5.

[54] Wheeler, Burton K., "*Yankee From the West*," Doubleday and Company, New York, 1962, page 423. Wheeler ran twice for president as a Socialist.

[55] Richards, page 95.

[56] Paid advertising, *Montana Standard*, Butte, Montana, 11/9/46.

[57] KOJM was the first "daytime only" station in Montana, KAVR was short lived and lasted about 18 months.

[58] *Broadcasting/Cablecasting Yearbook*, 1987 edition, pages B-172 through B-175.

[59] *The "M" Street Journal*, Houston, Texas, October 27, 1986.

[60] Information furnished by Tony Lopuch and Earl Crowder, engineers for KFBB, Great Falls, circa 1958.

[61] Paid advertising, *Montana Standard*, August 16, 1965, page 9.

[62] "*Montana, a State Guidebook*," Federal Writers Project, Viking Press, New York, 1939, page 438 (index).

[63] Brier and Blumberg, page 81.

[64] Richards, page 58. This was sometime before 1929 when KGCX moved to Wolf Point.

[65] Brier and Blumberg, page 81.

[66] Richards, page 60.

[67] "KOPR, Butte's New Radio Station," *Montana Standard*, Butte, Montana, June 9, 1948, page 5. The news article stated that KOPR was the first "ABC affiliate in Montana." KOPR was the first full-time affiliate of ABC.

[68] "*Everybody's Ideas Poems*," Z Bar Network, Butte, Montana, private publication, 1938, page 1.

[69] Personal reminiscences of the author, former Z Bar employee.

[70] KXLK was originally assigned the call sign KSTR, but never used it. *Farms Illustrated Magazine*, Pacific Northwest Broadcasters, Portland, Oregon, September 1946, page 28.

[72] "Wheelings and Dealings," op. cit.

[73] *Farms Illustrated*, op. cit., page 28.

[74] "*White's Radio Log*," Charles DeWitt White, Bronxville, New York, various issues, 1946 to 1950.

[75] Personal experiences of the author, former KGVO employee.

[76] *Broadcasting/Cablecasting Yearbook*, 1987 edition, page F-63.

[77] See both Richards and Brier and Blumberg sections on early day programming of Montana stations.

[79] A claim often made, but never proven by the KFBB management. Many stations in the Midwest made similar claims.

[80] The employee was reported working across town at KUDI the next week.

[81] Personal experiences of the author. Much of the information was acquired while an employee of KFBB, 1957-1961. The quote is attributed to former KFBB employee Art Weber, now a Great Falls businessman.

[82] *"Farms Illustrated,"* magazine, December 1946, page 24.

[83] *"Everybody's Ideas Poems,"* op. cit., frontpiece of booklet.

[84] *The Ed Craney Collection* in the Montana State Historical Library at Helena contains a wealth of information on the "Montana Boosters."

[85] Brier and Blumberg, page 79.

[86] Richards, page 24.

[87] ibid, page 29

[88] "KGIR, Blast of Sound," op. cit.

[89] The reader is referred to Richards' thesis for details.

[90] "KOPR, Butte's New Radio Station," Actually the newspaper article was vague concerning the actual station ownership. Some in Butte maintained the Anaconda Company was the main source of capital for KOPR.

[91] Record Group 173, *Federal Communications Commission* (Docket 10026). Montana State Historical Society Library, Helena.

[92] "Stay Tuned," pages 88 and 131.

[93] ibid, page 193.

[94] A "Blanket license" provides for the complete use of the music agency's library in return for a specified percentage of the station's annual gross.

[95] Personal experience of the author while an employee of both KGVO and KXLQ, the Z Bar Net station at Bozeman.

[96] ibid.

[97] *Broadcasting/Cablecasting Year Book*, op. cit.

[98] Personal conversation with Ethel Ehreshman, long-time employee of KGVW, Belgrade, Montana, December 6, 1984.

[99] *"Key Notes,"* a promotional magazine published for KEMC listeners, various issues.

[100] Brier and Blumberg, pages 87-89. KXLF-TV's studios were so small, the automobile commercials had to be shot on the street outside.

[101] "Kixlif," is the phonetic pronunciation for "KXLF."

[102] Brier and Blumberg, op. cit.

[103] "KYUS, Cayuse TV," *Montana Magazine*, Helena, Montana, Fall issue, 1976.

[104] *Broadcasting/Cablecasting Yearbook*, 1987 edition, page C-37.

[105] A quote generally attributed to W. C. "Bud" Blanchette, former executive for Western Broadcasting Company, Missoula and KFBB, Great Falls.

[106] "KGIR, Blast of Sound," pages 17-18.

[107] A quote from Dick Kober, former manager, KGHL, Billings.

[108] Personal communication, William Strothman (KBTK), Missoula, 1965.

[109] Several Montana broadcasters have made it to the "Big Time." They include: Don Oliver, former NBC newsman; Jack Bogut of Glasgow, now with stations in Pittsburgh, Pennsylvania and Donna Kelley, Jack Womack and Harley D. Hotchkiss, now with CNN in Atlanta. Reed Collins, formerly with CBS and now with CNN, worked for a while at KFBB in the 1940s.

[110] KGLE, Glendive, with a power of 500 watts, can be heard on a good receiver at Billings in the daytime due to high ground conductivity.

[111] Field tests conducted by the author in the Blackfoot Valley near Missoula and Ovando.

[112] Multipath signals are the equivalent of "ghosts" on TV. One or more signals from the same FM station will bounce off a hill or other object and arrive at the receiving antenna a fraction of a second later than the direct signal, causing distortion.

[113] The school's legal name is Montana College of Mineral Science and Technology. Eastern Montana College is now Montana State University/Billings.

[114] Personal correspondence, John C. Johnson, board operator at KTVQ (TV), Billings, July 9, 1991.

[115] A cross-section of opinion gleaned from conversations with various station managers during this time period.

[116] "25 years of Montana Gospel Radio," *Montana Christian*, Lewistown, Montana, January-February issue, 1986, page one.

[117] Ethel Ehreshman, op. cit.

[118] "25 Years," op. cit.

[119] "*The 'M' Street Journal*," Alexandria, Virginia, Volume 4, Number 15, April 13, 1987.

[120] Personal conversation with Fred "Fritz" Bartlett, Chief Engineer at KGHL, Billings, various dates, 1964-65.

[121] "KGIR, Blast of Sound," pages 17-18.

[122] "KSEN/KZIN, 30 years of Progress," supplement to the *Shelby Prompter* and *Cut Bank Pioneer Press*, August 1977.

[123] ibid.

[124] *Broadcasting/Cablecasting Yearbook*, 1987 edition, pages B-174 and B-175.

[125] Personal Conversation with Don. H. McDonald, consulting engineer, D-S-J Services, Kalispell, Montana, June 1987.

[126] Montana FM frequency assignment chart, *Broadcasting/Cablecasting Yearbook*, 1995 edition.

[127] *FCC Rules and Regulations*, section 74, subpart L.

[128] ibid., section 74, subpart G.

[129] Personal conversation with IMN personnel, Bozeman, Montana, October, 1985.

[130] FM stations have the capability of transmitting material either as supplemental programming or technical data on sub-channels (sidebands) that ride "piggyback" on the FM carrier. They cannot be heard without a special receiver.

[131] *Broadcasting/Cablecasting Yearbook*, 1987, Edition, pages B-172 through B-175.

[132] Gilles, T. J., "Live From Shelby," *Montana Magazine*, Helena, Montana, September, 1983, page 26. Gilles is a staff writer for the *Great Falls Tribune*. Quotes used by permission from T. J. Gilles, September, 1992.

[133] In past years, some Montana cable systems carried FM signals from out-of-state along with their digital "Cable radio" channels.

[134] Unpublished survey by the author among various Montana broadcasters, December, 1993.

[135] ibid.

[136] This entry is here only to see if anyone checks the footnotes.

[137] Based strictly on the author's experience, knowledge and his opinion! The Montana Broadcasters Association and Greater Montana Foundation have a "Broadcasters Hall of Fame" which is displayed in the Communications Buildings at Montana State University/Bozeman and the University of Montana at Missoula. This includes Ed Craney, Chet Huntley, Dale Moore and Joseph Sample.

[138] Huntley, Chet (Chester), "*The Generous Years*," Random House Publishing, New York, 1968.

[139] Poindexter, Raymond, "*Golden Throats and Silver Tongues*," River Road Press, Conway, Arkansas, 1978. Pages 107, 142, 149, 174 and 205.

[140] MacDonald, J. Fred, "*Don't Touch That Dial*," Nelson Hall Press, Chicago, 1979, pages 334, 349.

SPECIAL ACKNOWLEDGEMENT

To Michael A. Cornell, Assistant Manager of KMBI AM/FM, Spokane, Washington for assistance with the various charts, especially "The Growth of Broadcasting in Montana." Also, KMBI manager Gary Leonard graciously allowed the use of the station's recording equipment in the preparation of the audio cassette version of this treatise. CHM

+BIBLIOGRAPHY+

Blanchette, Willis C. "Bud," former executive, Western Broadcasting Company, Missoula, Montana. Personal quote, date unknown.

Brier, Warren J. and Blumberg, Nathan B. (editors), *A Century of Montana Journalism*, Mountain Press Publishing Company, Missoula, Montana, 1971.

Broadcasting/Cablecasting Yearbook, Broadcasting Publications, Washington, D.C., Various editions, 1987-1993.

Craney Collection, The Ed, Montana Historical Society Library, Helena, Montana. Also, cassette tapes furnished the author by E.B. Craney.

Dilley, Raymond G., "Montana's First TV Stations," *A Century of Montana Journalism*, Mountain Press Publishing Company, Missoula, Montana, 1971.

Ehreshman, Ethel, long-time employee of KGVW, Belgrade and the Enterprise Network, personal conversation, December 6, 1984.

"Everybody's Ideas Poems," Z Bar Network, private publication, Butte, Montana (circa 1938). Courtesy Ronald T. Warner, Billings, Montana.

Farms Illustrated Magazine, Pacific Northwest Broadcasters, Portland, Oregon, September and December issues, 1946. On file in Montana Historical Society Library at Helena.

F-C-C Rules and Regulations, Federal Communications Commission, Washington D.C., Section 74.

Federal Communications Commission (Docket 10026, Record Group 173, Montana Historical Society Library, Helena Montana

Federal Writers' Project, (Works Progress Adminstration), *Montana: A State Guidebook*, Viking Press, New York, 1939.

"Fire Destroys Downtown KGVO Plant," *Daily Missoulian*, Missoula, Montana, February 20, 1950.

Frost, S.S., *Education's Own Stations*, publisher unknown, Chicago, 1937.

Gilles, T.J., "Live From Shelby," *Montana Magazine*, Montana Magazine Publishing Company, Helena, Montana, September-October 1983.

"High Power Radio Opposed by Montana Broadcasters," *Great Falls Tribune*, Great Falls, Montana, March 9, 1948.

Huntley, Chet (Chester), *The Generous Years*, Random House Publishing, New York, 1978.

Jenkins, Thomas, Chief Engineer, KUSM-TV (Montana State University), Bozeman, Montana, personal conversation, March 1986.

"*Keynotes*," Promotional Newsletter published by KEMC, Eastern Montana College, Billings, Montana, various issues.

"KGIR: Blast of Sound Heard 'Round the Town,'" *Montana Standard*, Butte, Montana, March 11, 1979, page 17.

"KGVO Moves," *Sunday Missoulian*, Missoula, Montana, February 2, 1981. Paid advertising supplement. This article quoted extensively from the Richards' thesis with no credit given.

Kober, Richard "Dick," (deceased), former manager, KGHL, Billings, Montana, Personal conversation, March 1986.

"KOPR, Butte's New Radio Station," *Montana Standard*, Butte, Montana, June 9, 1948, page 5.

KSEN/KZIN, 30 Years of Progress," Newspaper supplement to *Shelby Prompter* and *Cut Bank Pioneer Press*, August 1977.

"KYUS, Cayuse TV, Miles City," *Montana Magazine*, Montana Magazine Publishing Company, Helena, Montana, fall issue, 1976.

Lang, William, editor, "*Montana, The Magazine of Western History*," Montana Historical Library, Helena, Montana, letter; February 1, 1985

"*M Street Journal, The*," Houston, Texas and Alexandria, Virginia, October 1986 through April 1987.

Malone, Michael P. and Roeder, Richard B., *Montana, A History of Two Centuries*, University of Washington Press, Seattle, 1977.

Masterson, Jim, "*It Happened in Montana*," Number 64, an historical cartoon series from the Greater Montana Foundation Collection. Courtesy Museum of The Rockies, Bozeman, Montana.

MacDonald, J. Fred, *Don't Touch That Dial*, Nelson Hall Press, Chicago 1979.

McDonald, Don H., Consulting engineer, D-S-J Broadcast Technical Services, Kalispell, Montana. Personal communication, June 1987.

"*Montana, A Directory of Newspapers and Radio Stations*," Montana Department of Labor and Industry, Naegle Printing, Helena, Montana, 1938.

Patterson, Mrs. W.H., commercial manager, KOFI, Kalispell, Montana, Telephone conversation, November 8, 1983.

Poindexter, Ray, "*Golden Throats and Silver Tongues*," River Road Press, Conway Arkansas.

Richards, Ron(ald) P., "*A History of Radio Broadcasting in Montana*," Masters thesis, University of Montana, Missoula, 1963.

_____"Montana's Pioneer Radio Stations," A Century of Montana Journalism, Mountain Press Publishing Company, Missoula, Montana, 1971.

Riggins, George, "Radio at the Old Alma Mater (author)," *Radio World Magazine*, Falls Church, Virginia, November 8, 1989, page 26.

Snyder, Dan, manager KCAP/KZMT, Helena, Montana, personal conversation, September 6, 1986.

Sterling, Christopher H. and Kittross, John M., *Stay Tuned, A Concise History of American Broadcasting*, Wadsworth Publishing, Belmont, California, 1978.

Strothman, William "Bill," former manager, KBTK, Missoula, Montana, personal conversation, 1963.

Special Collections Division, Renne Library, Montana State University, Bozeman. File on broadcast stations.

Survey of Montana Broadcasters, unpublished material, October 1983.

"Twenty-five Years of Montana Gospel Radio," *Montana Christian (newspaper)*, Lewistown, Montana, January-February issue, 1986.

"Two Babes Grow Up," *Montana Standard*, Butte, Montana, Sunday March 11, 1979. Feature article.

Walton, Lyman B., (deceased) personal conversation, Bozeman, circa 1950.

Warner, Ronald T., Longtime Montana announcer and newsman, various conversations and correspondence, 1974 through 1990.

Wheeler, Burton K., "*Yankee From the West*," Doubleday and Company New York, 1962.

"Wheelings and Dealings Dot Road Trod by Radio," *Montana Standard*, Butte, Montana, March 11, 1979.

White, T.H., "Broadcast Station Pioneers," Broadcast Forum, Compuserve Services, January 1, 1992.

White's Radio Log, Charles DeWitt White, Providence Rhode Island, various issues, 1946 to 1950.

Wolf Point Herald, Wolf Point, Montana, April 16, 1929.

+ABOUT THE AUTHOR+

C Howard "Howie" McDonald was born at Bozeman, Montana and grew up on a farm in Madison County, near Harrison. At a young age, he expressed an avid interest in radio, much to the dismay of his parents.

Following High School graduation at Bozeman, he became an apprentice at KXLQ, moving on to KGVO at Missoula and thence a tour of duty in the United States Air Force during the Korean Conflict where he studied electronics and subsequently taught in that career field. He attained the rank of Staff Sergeant.

After his military commitment, McDonald was announcer/program director at KFBB, Great Falls and later at KGVO. He also managed KRBN at Red Lodge and was later program director for KGHL and KURL, Billings.

After several years with WCTS, WPBC and WAYL (all FM) in Minneapolis; KXEL, Waterloo, Iowa, along with KWFC and KTTS, Springfield, Missouri, he returned to Montana to KGVW and was later news director at Bozeman's KBOZ. He has also worked for KBLG, Billings; KMBI AM/FM, Spokane and as an instructor at the American School of Broadcast at Spokane.

He is president of BIG M Broadcast Services, a broadcast engineering program consulting and publishing business.

He and his lovely wife, June, have four grown children and three delightful grandchildren.

McDonald is an avid cave explorer, outdoorsman and geneological researcher. A licensed broadcast engineer, he holds membership in the National Speleological Society, Baptist Bible College (MO) Alumni, the Gallatin County Historical Society and Sons of Conferderate Veterans. He has been called the "Walking Encyclopedia of Montana Broadcasting."

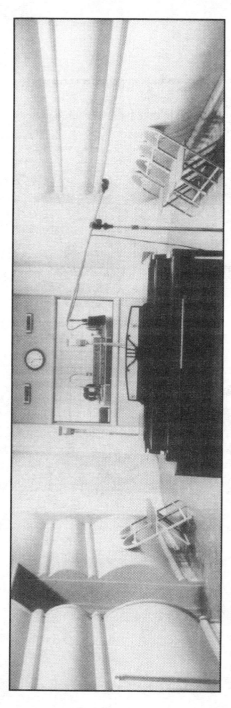

Main broadcast studio, typical of the late 1940's. News, drama and live musical programs originated from studios such as this. The lay-out and design is practically identical to the original KOPR (AM) studios in Butte's Finlen hotel. Courtesy American Radio Brokers, San Francisco.

Author at the controls of KFBB radio, Great Falls, April 1958.
Even at that time, most of the station's equipment was obsolete.

The original KPRK studio building east of Livingston. KPRK was one of the first post World War II stations and still operates from the same building, on its original frequency and with the same call letters.

Taken in the Spring of 1947 by the author.

The KFBB Radio-TV center west of Great Falls on Old Highway 89. The building burned to the ground in 1967. The land is now used as the KEIN (AM) transmitter site.

Taken in the 1960's by the author.

RADIO, TECHNOLOGY already was undergoing continuing refinements when KGIR, Butte's first radio station, moved from Shiner's Furniture Store to 121 W. Broadway around 1929. The new studio was in what once was mining mogul W.A. Clark's office. Craney was told roll-up metal fire doors in the office were installed because Clark liked his privacy. A huge piece of native silver that had

KGIR: Blast of sound heard

Libby's First Radio Station Completes Final Tests, Technical Arrangements; 12½ Hours' Daily Schedule Is Planned

Climaxing more than 12 months of arduous work a planning KLCB, Libby's own radio station, will begin broacasting on a regular schedule Saturday morning, Decemb 2, at 6:30 o'clock.

Programs will then be broadcast daily, inch from 6:30 a.m. to 10:35 a.m. G. Cohen. Great Falls, ored for producing the Radio day n "Special Program Series" prod- tii Program of the Year for its nno duced by Michael Grant the Awards were presented in the fo rants,

The following categories: — TV Station of the Year — assigne KOOK-TV, Billings, Vic Miller, cycles, —Honorable mention—KRTV, power o. Great Falls, Cliff Ewing. ƒ The st. Radio Station of the Year— well as t. KYLT, Missoula, Gene Peter- company son. Creek Roac —Honorable mention—KXLO, power plant Lewistown, Joseph Zahler. Libby City —TV Program of the Year— The station No first prize awarded. persons consi —2nd — KXLF-TV, Butte, Coburn, manag Richard eer; Mary Elizab "Let's Talk to ..." program directo Maney. sportscaster events

High Power Radio Opposed By Montana Broadcasters

HELENA, March 8 (UP)—The Montana Association of Broadcasters today was on record in active support of a bill introduced in congress by Sen. Edwin C. Johnson of do to limit the power of ra-to 50,000 watts. ion meeting here repre--sters.

asking Montana's congressional delegation to call upon members of the senate interstate and foreign commerce committee to urg speedy hearings on the bill and that members of the delegation suppor and vote for the bill on the floor of congress. The bill was introduced "to provide more equitable radio service to the various communities of the States and to prevent mon association's resolutio

(those abov olution said to many in tations, plac jeopardy e riving them o riving listener o service. ions in only would "concer dk number of indi poly of greater eco L; and social powe entrusted in any in oup in a free nation. said. a not enough frequer try community or eve s to have a super-powe the resolution declarec granting of super-powe station or stations in th States is a policy matter t rmined by congress—not a ering matter."

Montana association will a / support and seek passage c son's bill. I on Treloar of KGEZ, Kalispe s elected president of the ass ation. Paul McAdam of KPR Livingston w finished secretary.

Radio Station KLTZ Goes On Air In Glasgow

New Local Enterprise ' Broadcast At 1240; F Of Remote Control Ty

gow's new radio had its official or o.m. today, the o t. Official clear th- shington com n was receiv

KGCX Celebrates 20th Anniversary

ONE of the great pio in Montana is ab anniversary — ed for oper power o. half o

radio stations rate its 20th 'CX. Owned 'as licens. 1926 with

people! 929, the munications authorized a Wolf Point, Montana and also grant. increase in power to 250 watts. Radio ucasti those days was one continual round of un-will be fi usual experiences. Owing to the lack of tele-possibly the fi phone facilities in the vast trade area sur-to operate e rounding Wolf Point, the station soon be-control. came an "angel of r to everyone on the Mr. Scofie move! In the d. ter, farmers and several mon of equipmer ranchers wh- o drive to Wolf transmitter Point on zards raging out gow. ing e ny miles of Asse

Ed Krebsbach Manager KGCX

Pioneer of radio era

naff, ve neces- gwo additional eers with- the -CC first-class radio-telephone operator's license. He let it be known that he is now on the lookout for such caliber of radiomen, adding that if ther anyone in the county at — filling those qual terested in — cont—

University Lists Radio, TV Awards

Great Falls Tribune   Sunday, May 21, 1972

MISSOULA (AP) — The Uni- —Honorable mention—KYLT, versity of Montana Foun- Missoula, "New Year's Party dation Radio-TV Awards Satur- Line Special," Louie Nordbye. day naming KOOK-TV, Billings —Honorable mention—KGVO, the TV Station of the Year and Missoula, "The Little Big KYLT, Missoula, as Radio Sta- Horn," Tom McGinley. tion of the Year. —Radio-TV Idea of the Year— eleventh annual awards —KFBB-TV, Great Falls, place honors Peterson. Dunham. —Honorable mention—KYLT, Missoula, "Hess' Heroes," Gene —able mention—KBOW Montana

the 1971 Great Montana presented Butte, "Christmas Show," Gerri Steward. —Announcer of the Year — Ernest Hopseker, KCAP, Hel ena. —Honorable mention — Dave Mack, KGVO, Missoula. —Copywriter of the Year — Carol Shepherd, KYLT, Mis soula. —Honorable mention — Linda Madson, KLTZ, Glasgow. —Honorable mention — Bar bara Leland, KBLL, Helena. —and radio network Montana.

music.

CRANEY'S STINT as advertising manager for his high school paper propelled him into that era. An advertiser who ran an aviation school "apparently liked the way I tried to sell." He asked Craney about his plans. "I said I was going to work in the woods someplace, then go to Washington State College. My mother wanted me to become a doctor. I wanted to become an electrical engineer. He offered me a job in his (radio parts) store." Craney got a broom and cleaned out the shop, told the

at five Swan Lake, then an ached by steamboat. ght other youngsters ber camp had a tutor became Craney's v. His next teacher er, then just out of

days, you didn't w much to teach." raney has written and given to the state historical library in Helena a story of his years at Swan Lake, times that

To order additional copies of **"Voices in the Big Sky!"**, complete the information below.

Ship to: (please print)

Name _____

Address _____

City, State, Zip _____

Day phone _____

_____ copies of **BOOK** @ $12.95 each $ _____

_____ copies of **BOOK ON TAPE** (voiced by Author) @ $12.95 each $ _____

Postage and handling @ $4.00 per **BOOK/BOOK ON TAPE** $ _____

Total amount enclosed $ _____

Make checks payable to BIG M Broadcast Services

Send to: *Howard McDonald c/o Big M Broadcast Services*
P.O. Box 1672 • Bozeman, MT 59715

To order additional copies of **"Voices in the Big Sky!"**, complete the information below.

Ship to: (please print)

Name _____

Address _____

City, State, Zip _____

Day phone _____

_____ copies of **BOOK** @ $12.95 each $ _____

_____ copies of **BOOK ON TAPE** (voiced by Author) @ $12.95 each $ _____

Postage and handling @ $4.00 per **BOOK/BOOK ON TAPE** $ _____

Total amount enclosed $ _____

Make checks payable to BIG M Broadcast Services

Send to: *Howard McDonald c/o Big M Broadcast Services*
P.O. Box 1672 • Bozeman, MT 59715